Debotri Dhar teaches Women's Studies at the University of Michigan. Her books, scholarly as well as fiction, include *Postcards from Oxford: Stories of Women and Travel* (London), the novel *The Courtesans of Karim Street* (New Delhi), *The Best Asian Short Stories 2018* (Singapore; selected and edited with introduction), *Education and Gender* (Bloomsbury: New York, London; edited with introduction), and others. Her shorter fiction has been published in literary magazines and anthologies worldwide. Debotri is the founder of the Hummingbird Global Writers' Circle, a transnational travelling literary initiative to foster a love of books, cultural exchange, and global understanding.

Debotri earned a Bachelors' degree in Economics from Delhi University, a Masters' in Women's Studies, with distinction, from Oxford University and her PhD in Women's and Gender Studies from Rutgers University.

AF647091

LOVE IS NOT A WORD

The Culture and Politics of Desire

EDITED BY DEBOTRI DHAR

SPEAKING TIGER

SPEAKING TIGER BOOKS LLP
4381/ 4, Ansari Road, Daryaganj
New Delhi 110002

First published in paperback by Speaking Tiger Books 2020

Anthology Copyright © Speaking Tiger 2020
Essays Copyright © Individual contributors 2020

The essay, 'Swipe Me Left, I'm Dalit' by Christina Dhanaraj, p. 57, was first published in an abbreviated version by GenderIT.Org, a project of the Women's Rights Programme of the Association for Progressive Communication, and is reproduced here with their permission.

ISBN: 978-93-89958-30-0
eISBN: 978-93-89958-31-7

10 9 8 7 6 5 4 3 2 1

The moral right of the author has been asserted.

Typeset in Sabon Roman by SÜRYA, New Delhi
Printed at Chaman Enterprises, New Delhi

All rights reserved.

No part of this publication may be reproduced, transmitted, or stored in a retrieval system, in any form or by any means, electronic, mechanical, photocopying, recording or otherwise, without the prior permission of the publisher.

This book is sold subject to the condition that it shall not, by way of trade or otherwise, be lent, resold, hired out, or otherwise circulated, without the publisher's prior consent in any form of binding or cover other than that in which it is published.

Contents

Introduction vii
Debotri Dhar

Perspectives on Indian Love: *Swayamvara*, Arranged Marriage, and *Desi* Romance 1
Malashri Lal

Radha, Divine Paramour 16
Makarand R. Paranjape

Love, Longing, and Desire: A *Nayika's* Tale 41
Alka Pande

Swipe Me Left, I'm Dalit 57
Christina Dhanaraj

Love Jihad 67
Nilanjan Mukhopadhyay

Ghalib's Poetic Beloved: Cruel, Willful, and Elusive 87
Mehr Afshan Farooqi

Love, Society, Polity: Urdu Poetry from Khusro to Faiz 98
Zafar Anjum

Barahmasa: Songs for the Seasons of Love and Separation 114
Rakhshanda Jalil

Single Women, Self-love, and the Gender of Waiting 126
Debotri Dhar

Same-sex Love in India 144
Parvati Sharma

How to Write a Love Letter to a Tree 158
Sumana Roy

Love and the City 169
Didier Coste

Notes 186
Bibliography 204
About the Contributors 207

Introduction

DEBOTRI DHAR

The idea for this book first occurred to me when I was a graduate student at Oxford University; and then again, a couple of years and another continent later, while teaching at Rutgers University in the United States. Why, I wondered, while watching the leaves change colour in the fall, were there very few serious yet engaging books on love, its many moods and multiple meanings? Just when I was considering taking a writing break to head to Kasauli, that misty, much-loved haunt in the Himalayas, life took me to teach at a liberal arts college in Ohio for a year. The cottages, rolling hills, and winding country roads in that part of America were not entirely unlike those in Kasauli in India, the horse-and-buggies of the Amish community adding an extra touch of Midwestern whimsy. But a full research and teaching schedule did mean that this book of essays—'somewhat unusual,' in the delightfully measured words of an editor—remained a dream. It was only after I started teaching at the University of Michigan in Ann Arbor that various pieces of 'the love book,' as family and friends had fondly started referring to it, began to fall in place. A long gestation indeed...

This is a collection of twelve essays on love by scholars, critics, essayists, and journalists. Love: at once art, insight, event, encounter, aporia, utopia, ethic. In literature, culture, history, metaphysics, politics, and their interstices, ideas about love abound. Love has been a central mood and metaphor in fiction, poetry, and drama around the world: Shakespeare's *Romeo and Juliet*, for instance, or *Antony and Cleopatra*. Or *Gone with the Wind*, Margaret Mitchell's 1936 American novel that went on to be captured exquisitely on celluloid: Vivian Leigh and Clark Gable, love's lessons, love's loss, no less than a saga and no more than a light shrug—'Frankly, my dear, I don't give a damn.' And how could we forget the many visions and revisions of love in Sanskrit classics such as Sudraka's play *Mrcchakatika* (The Little Clay Cart); and the fifth century poet Kalidasa's lyric poem *Meghduta* (The Cloud Messenger) which narrates how, in the wet, quivering season of *asadha*, a *yaksa* exiled in Ramagiri entreats a passing rain-cloud to carry his message of love to his beloved left behind in the ancient Indian city of Alaka?

In the first essay in this collection, '*Swayamvara*, Arranged Marriage, and *Desi* Romance,' Malashri Lal offers some fascinating perspectives on 'Indian love,' mapping both continuity and change, possibility and paradox. Drawing from sources as diverse as epics like the *Ramayana* and the *Mahabharata* that continue to hold sway over the collective imagination, works of literature including those by women writers from the Indian diaspora in the United States, and Bollywood films, Lal asks if from ancient to modern times, the principle of a woman's choice in love and marriage has ever been entirely absent any more than it has ever been fully realized. Rather than monolithically posit the 'powerlessness' of Indian women against the imperial-colonial assumption of 'freedom' of her Western counterpart, Lal's essay thus draws our attention to the many diversities that constitute India's spectrum—international designer wedding ensembles for the rich and child marriages among the very poor, the stark portrayals of love in a consumerist global media versus the textured layers of everyday life—to underscore the complexity, the 'in-betweenness,' the being and becoming of love.

We turn, then, to 'divine love' and its myriad depictions across literatures and cultures. The 1977 Australian classic, *Thornbirds* by Colleen McCullough, for instance, a complex tale of a man torn between his love of a woman and his love of Christ. Returning to the Indian context, Lal's discussion of love and women's choice in Indian epics, her brief invocation of Gandhi, and her critique of the imperial gaze overlap in intriguing ways with the second essay in the collection by Makarand Paranjape. Paranjape's essay on immortal love focuses on the 'lover-God' Krishna and his consort Radha, 'a milkmaid elevated to the status of the erotic and holy beloved of the Supreme Godhead.'

According to Paranjape, the extraordinary story of Radha must be read not just for itself, but in the larger context of Indian history, art, culture, and metaphysics. The male-dominated Hindu theology of Vaishnavism before Radha suffered from a Goddess-lack and this, Paranjape argues, is why the Vaishnava revival and even female-dominant Shaktism needed the love-Goddess Radha. Hardly mentioned in classical sources and scriptures such as the *Bhagavata Purana* but later assuming prominence in Jayadev's *Gitagovinda*, Radha's importance as Krishna's chosen paramour, even spouse, steadily rises, her persona being further moulded by poets like Chandidas, Vidyapati, and Surdas. Paranjape traces Radha's metamorphosis under the puritanical gaze of colonial modernity, and how her passionate dalliance with Krishna became an embarrassment to the agenda of political and social reform espoused by the proponents of Hindu respectability. Hence this essay's ultimate philosophical and provocative speculation: what would Radha say to Mahatma Gandhi, if she were suddenly to meet him as he was trying to rid himself of all sexual passions for the sake of society and polity?

The theme of the cultural erasure of sexuality through a resurgent respectability politics is carried forward in the next essay by Alka Pande, which re-engages with the *Kamasutra* through the eyes of the famed *nayika* and *nagarvadhu* of Pataliputra, Amrapali. Told in the voice of this powerful courtesan who, in desiring as well as being desired, chooses her men and 'lives her life independently, not subjugating herself to any man,' the essay gives us a postcolonial glimpse into an exquisitely imagined past, and even an unlikely foreshadowing of feminist futures.

In *A Lover's Discourse*, the French literary theorist and philosopher Roland Barthes also spoke of romantic love's artful un-anchoring, the language of lovers that punctures quotidian narratives tying us to social worlds, dulled times and spaces, to permit a gentle haemorrhage that makes anything possible.[1] Yet, love can be as much about passion as about power, about politics. In *Methodology of the Oppressed*, postcolonial feminist Chela Sandoval powerfully interrogated the narrative form of 'falling in love' and the predominance of a Western ethic of romantic love 'where love becomes law.'[2] Drawing from the work of those such as Barthes, Sandoval examined power, social and psychic emancipation, a hermeneutic of love-as-consciousness.

So what about the trying, troubled, less-than-luminous shades of love? Barthes, too, had formulated love as that 'place of life' between narrative forms, 'a marked and wounded space, a site of shifting.'[3] Yes, love's wounds can bleed profusely when they strike against law and life. Elsewhere I have written about the race and caste of love in the United States and India respectively, and how

> [D]uring periods of racial segregation, there were laws penalizing 'miscegenation' or inbreeding between racial groups; and while much has changed, much has not. Interracial marriage—especially based on mutual respect rather than fetishization—is certainly more acceptable now, at least in some spaces, but it would be impossible to argue that it is the norm in America. This is similar to inter-caste love marriage in India; once considered taboo in orthodox circles, the stranglehold of caste norms may have weakened in some ways but remain as stubborn, as irresolute, in others. While writing my thesis that combined theoretical perspectives on education and empowerment with everyday manifestations in public culture, the latter including matrimonial advertisements in newspapers, it was saddening to see that the formal degrees of the educated did not always stop them from seeking a partner from the same caste. Marriage, in other words, has often functioned as a tool to enforce race and caste endogamy, to preserve the 'purity' of groups, and maintain hierarchy.[4]

The next two essays examine precisely such troubling aspects of the politics of love and desire. Christina Dhanaraj's essay uses a Dalit feminist lens to shed light on the romantic experiences of Dalit women who have to bear the double burden of caste and gender, not unlike the race and gender burden borne by women of colour in the West. Critiquing the savarna gaze of Indian cultural iconography for its stereotyping of Dalit identities on one hand, and elite feminist discussions of women's sexuality and sex positive cultural politics on the other, the essay highlights how liberal lifestyle alternatives practiced by mainstream Indian feminists who come from privileged social locations could potentially be more exploitative for Dalit women.

Nilanjan Mukhopadhyay's essay examines love in the context of politicized religion: inter-faith love marriages in India, and the 'love-jihad' campaign. Love and jihad are incompatible words per se; but Mukhopadhyay traces how some members of Hindutva, Islamist, and other religious groups have used the two words, 'one after the other and in the same sequence, by treating the two as different parts of speech,' and as part of an insidious politics. Thus, Hindu men were exhorted to protect their culture and their women from the alleged Muslim 'love-jihadis', these allegations not just exerting a decisive impact on politics in north India, but whose rumbles have also been heard in some Muslim dominated districts of south India. Mukhopadhyay demonstrates how allegations of love jihad continue to be traded between various religious communities, with a Catholic Bishop recently alleging that Christian girls were being 'abducted by Love Jihad'—but this time by a Hindu outfit, to destroy 'Christian essence'. What has this patriarchal politics of love-jihad—'our' women, 'their' women—meant for the women whose bodies and religion it claims to protect?

This is the darker side of love, not just as it bestows life but as it bequeaths suffering. Yes, love can be a wound, as seen also in suicide notes that testify not to love's joys but to how deception and violence in the name of love resulted in suicide, where God is invoked as the court of last resort, holding out indefinite punishment for a *sin*, in the language of faith, where secular courts could not be depended upon to award definite punishment for a *crime* in the language of law.[5] And yet, while one's personal faith may offer both inspiration and consolation, organized religion's role in serving as an ideological and institutional means for controlling gendered bodies cannot be denied. For instance, the raped female body being framed as unchaste and irreversibly shamed has sometimes resulted in the ending of life itself. Elsewhere too, I have studied this dual relationship between feminism, faith, and love that might be read alongside the above two perspectives on religion by Paranjape and Mukhopadhyay.[6] My work questioned why the antagonistic positing of feminism against religious faith—even *all* faiths—has to be the only solution for advocates of social justice. What about alternative theoretical, cultural, and lived interpretations of the question of faith and feminism, given that the global ubiquity of gender violence transcends the left-right and religious-secular divides, and exposes the limitations of both law and Western liberal theory? Instead, might we need a combination of just faith, just law, just love?

Love: more than pursuit, less than perfection. No collection of essays on love could possibly be complete without a tribute to the Urdu *ghazal* and its poetic rendering of love through the boudoirs and boulevards of time. Mehr Afshan Farooqi's essay studies Urdu poetry's famous exponent Mirza Ghalib and his ideas of the beloved: the beloved as dark-skinned ('her long hair is dark and dense, and her body reflects the blackness of the tresses' such that the dark woman is presented as more enticing), as gendered or genderless, human or God. Farooqi traces the evolution of the *ghazal*, arguing that Ghalib's love for arcane Persian notwithstanding, the literary form and aesthetics of his poetry also displays very local colours and cultural characteristics, as seen in his delightful intermixing of tropes, linguistic juxtapositions, derivations from Sanskrit, and poetic imageries like that of an Indian beauty bathing in the rose garden and drying her hair among the Persian hyacinths.

Love, then, is both personal and political. The next essay by Zafar Anjum examines love in Urdu *shayari* beyond Ghalib and romance. Reminding us that Urdu poetry has many forms—*nazm, ghazal, qasida, masnavi, marsia* and *rubai*—the essay travels back in time, to early poets like Amir Khusro, Quli Qutub Shah and Wali, as well as forward, to Urdu poetry's 'last towering practitioner', Faiz Ahmed Faiz. In-between are the oeuvres of other poets such as Sauda, Mir, Ghalib, Daagh, Zauq, Hasrat, and Iqbal. Anjum thus pays obeisance to a long line of poets who dipped their flaming quills in both passion and politics, addressing larger themes such as empire, nationhood, Sufism, mass movements, modernity, and the market.

Alongside these expressions of love in and through 'high' culture—the classical, the textual, the urban, the masculine—counter cultures have also existed, and even thrived. Rakhshanda Jalil's essay explores the *barahmasa*—rural and oral songs for twelve months of the year, narrating the pain of separation from the beloved—and how it was counterpoised against the textuality and classicism of the *ghazal*. The essay also reminds us that though the *barahmasa* as a genre emerges as a counter narrative in that it foregrounded women's voices, needs, and desires (*zenana boli*), it was ultimately written by male composers.

While the *barahmasa* did not have risqué jokes and ribald innuendo, unlike *rekhti* poetry, instead focusing on the *virahini* pining for her lover, would these idealized images of pining women be somewhat altered if women were allowed to be the authors of their own lives / loves rather than being imagined through the male gaze, howsoever sympathetic the latter might be?

Would the *gender* of love be different?

Barthes had said, 'The lover's fatal identity is precisely this: I am the one who waits.' But what is the gender of this 'I' of love's (in)decisions, love's choices, even love's waiting? My essay in this collection examines the relationship between love, waiting, and gender. As the essay argues, 'even a cursory glance at literatures, broadly defined to include fables, fairy-tales, literary and popular fiction, poetry and drama, reveals that traditionally, it was the woman who waited for the man—for the father, husband, and sons she loved—to return from work, or war, while tending lovingly to the home and hearth.' In literatures from around the world, including *bhasha* literatures from India, are there as many instances of men waiting for love when women leave? What forms might the leaving and waiting for love take today, with marriage being delayed or even rejected by women in order to pursue work, vocation, art? Can the self-love of single women also be seen as liberating, and a creative site of resistance?

Not surprisingly, these challenges for heterosexual love and its representations in literature, law and society have been compounded manifold when it comes to same-sex love. In her sensitive essay on same-sex love in India, Parvati

Sharma writes of private love, despair—and always, hope—against the public backdrop of the decades-old legal battle around Section 377 of the Indian Penal Code. The essay draws on personal experience alongside literary writings on homosexuality, LGBTQ+ activist material, and judicial judgments, including the Supreme Court's recent progressive ruling on Section 377 and on privacy as a fundamental right. Privacy, for Sharma, is not just a postulate of law, or of bedrooms; she speaks, instead, of the privacy of ecstasy, and of the unsettling nature of 'love without the trappings that turn private ecstasy into social routine—marriage, family, children.' Sharma's essay, like others in the collection, ultimately alludes to the messy and paradoxical nature of romantic love itself, whose fluidity, sentimentality, and (il)logic cannot always be contained by the public-private and other neat binaries we variously inherit and inhabit.

And what if this illogic takes love's quest to unlikely, even if not unfamiliar, spaces? To trees, for instance, given the rich body of literature, including folktales, myths and metaphors, on romantic love between humans and trees? Sharanya Manivannan's prose-poem comes to mind here, with its opening line: I want a Boyfriend Like a Banyan Tree. 'A man who's a forest unto himself, with conspiracies of birds, and secret blossoms, and shaded places…And into this forest I will wander, a beloved of the world, and walk beneath the aegis of his boughs knowing that the same love that roots them raises me…I'll taste the rain from his bark and the wind from his stranglers and invent a susurrus language…I'll braid my hair into his and merge into his meditation, safe and gently swaying.'[7]

Sumana Roy's essay abandons the familiar rituals of human love to enter this world of tree-love. There are advantages to wooing trees, we are told; trees hold no grudges, and provide a respite from the unending expectations of human lovers. But here too, the relationship must be inaugurated with a love letter, which implies 'the invention of a new language, a new visual mimetic alphabet—the representation of trees through the shapes of their trunks and branches, new syntax, new grammar.' Also, writing a declaration of love on paper seems embarrassing to Roy, for paper is made from trees; the equivalent would be using 'human hide to write a love note to a lover.' There are other challenges such as reciprocity, the foundation of romantic love. A desire to convert one-sided love for plants into a dialogue, Roy conjectures, was what made the biologist Jagadish Chandra Bose turn to science, comparing plant behaviour with the human heart and devising instruments to get plants to write their autobiographies, their own love letters. Here we also learn that Melbourne residents have been writing romantic letters to their favourite trees ('You're very pretty' to an Algerian Oak, for instance), thereby gendering even their tree-lovers.

Whether between humans or with plants, the promise of love thus seems as socially constructed, and just as (im)possible. Didier Coste's essay takes us through some city fictions of love, from Gustave Flaubert's *Madame Bovary* in Rouen, and Proust's Swann and Odette, to Christina Stead's *Seven Poor Men of Sydney*, Peter Carey's *Oscar and Lucinda*, through Buenos Aires with Ernesto Sábato, Istanbul with Orhan Pamuk, and Delhi with Khushwant Singh's *Bhagmati*. For Coste, love and space are inseparable: 'Whatever happens in Verona is conditioned by the street and the piazza, the existence or not of secret and secluded places within walled city limits, balconies and dance halls, bedrooms with open doors and sacristies with closed ones.' Each city with its many lives, 'August's Rome and Nero's Rome, the Pope's Rome and Fellini's Roma,' can be 'anthropomorphized and even gendered…making it easier for the male gaze to fantasize its femininity, whether as a courtesan, a femme fatale, or a mother.' In undergoing constant metamorphosis, modern cities like Delhi thus become 'a parallel object of attachment, desire, nostalgia or repulsion, a rival for God and the rulers, a mirror of the beloved or an antagonist for the lover.' Hence, we are presented with an intriguing proposition, that 'the djinns, ghosts, nasty *bhoots* or the nicer elves haunt modern cities because there is nobody to feed them in the decrepit towers where the last locked-up princesses died of love-sickness and boredom when the first metro line opened in Delhi.'

Howsoever faintly we might hear echoes of the ancient in the modern, this much at least is true: the complex interrelationships of love and desire with time and space, with human, plant and the divine, and across law, literature and politics, do bring us back full circle, reminding us once again of the complexities, in-betweenness, the being and becoming of love.

*

My vision for this book was to commission essays on a variety of engaging perspectives on love that could nevertheless be threaded into a collection. Some of the essays are more scholarly, and others more personal. While each essay is stand-alone such that the reader can begin anywhere rather than only at the beginning, some may also be read together. For instance, Makarand Paranjape's essay on divine love and Nilanjan Mukhopadhyay's on 'love jihad' both engage, albeit in very different ways, with the intersections of love and religion; Mehr Farooqi's and Zafar Anjum's essays are on various shades of love in Urdu poetry; and Rakhshanda Jalil's essay on the Barahmasa, Parvati Sharma's essay on same-sex love, and mine on single women, self-love, and the gender of waiting, each examines different aspects of love and gender. Most of the essays have an Indian and Subcontinental focus; however, given my own journey, as well as how regional insularities can prove counter-productive beyond a point, I have attempted to ensure that the volume as a whole is also in conversation with 'Western' and transnational ideas and discourses.

Then, a troubling thought: can we speak of love without also speaking of war? Is war love's nemesis, its opponent and archrival, or merely another heightened shade and unseemly shadow of love? Here one is reminded of the book *Righteous Republic*'s juxtaposition of Rabindranath Tagore and Bankim Chandra Chattopadhyay, two Indian novelists and political thinkers who were utterly unlike each other in their approaches to love.[8] The book posits how Rabindranath the internationalist flatly opposed the telos of the nation-state, his romantic imagination 'devoid of the facticity and fatality of war', but that war was important to Bankim, whose god was the warrior-statesman Krishna rather than the cowherd-lover Krishna, his battle cry 'Bande Mataram' and his imagined community excluding the Other; and yet, the author argues, Rabindranath and Bankim 'both make Bengal, they both love Bengal.'[9] Would our collection have benefited from an insightful essay on war, perhaps drawing from work such as that of Chicana feminist scholar Gloria Anzaldua to frame love/war as *la frontera*, a crossroads, a suturing together of ruptured histories, memory, fences and barbed wires?[10] Or is it just as well that a collection on love ultimately has no essay on war?

Whatever may be its limitations for now, one hopes that this book will have much to offer its audience. As the curator and volume editor, it has already given me enough to think through—especially when I have found myself agreeing or disagreeing with this or that argument—along with also bringing incredible joys and eccentric pleasures.

The essays on Urdu poetry, for instance, rekindled ancient memories of Ghalib and Faiz, tomes pulled out of dusty shelves in remembrance of old promises, the dawns and dusks in different parts of the world made more beautiful through poetry. Snacking on fruit and cheese at an American eatery in Ann Arbor while reading Farooqi's interpretations of the Indic-Persian crossovers in Mirza Ghalib's oeuvre, the essay's highlighting of an intriguing poetic twist—the word *tale* (below) derived from the Sanskrit *tal* in Ghalib's '*radif ke tale*'—made me swallow an indignant olive in delight. Afterwards, walking home from the library on a snowy evening, down Liberty Street and through the colourful shops of Nickel's Arcade, the mind replayed many such literary and linguistic juxtapositions on love acquired over the years, whether Amir Khusro's exquisite romantic coupling of Persian and Sanskrit in '*Zihale maskeen makun taghaful duraye naina banaye batiyaan / sakhi piya ko jo main na dekhun, toh kaise kaatoon andheri ratiyaan,*' or that old Hindi film number on love with Amitabh Bachhan and Zeenat Aman rowing across gliding waters: '*amore mio dove stai tu sto cercando, sei solo mio amore mio / do lafzon ki hai dil ki kahaani...*' Paranjape's musings on divine love brought me face-to-face, for the millionth time, with Radha, whom I have often written about, whether as academic engagement or as fictional reinterpretation. And

Coste's essay travelling through Sydney, Pompei, Buenos Aires, Istanbul, and Delhi reminded me of my own journeys, its ruminations on love and the city making me see old spaces with new eyes, the silent serenades of present and absent lovers, elves under awnings and *bhoots* peeking out of manholes, truly a return of the repressed.

No, the world is not a 'global village'—the politics undergirding that kind of Universalist, homogenizing fantasy, and the discourses of love historically conditioned only by Western, White and imperialist brands of humanism, will forever remain suspect—and cultures can often be opaque to outsiders. But neither can our world be reductively reduced to discrete entities entirely impervious to travel, encounter, dialogue, love. How fascinating to think that the first time I had *mehndi* applied on my palms was not in India but in America, its dark, beautiful stains a testimony to our intersecting worlds, their mutating geographies and constantly colliding histories. It is to those intersections that the book is dedicated.

I dedicate this book, also, to its contributors and readers. For Renuka Chatterjee of Speaking Tiger Books and for Tahira Thapar's inputs; the fellowship provided by Michigan's Center for the Education of Women, and for the Center's supportive ex-Director Dr. Gloria Thomas; for the University of Michigan's Women's Studies program and our students; for my family, always; and for anyone who has contributed their ideas and affection to this book, from around the globe, my gratitude and much love.

Dr. Debotri Dhar

January 2020,

Ann Arbor, Michigan

Perspectives on Indian Love

Swayamvara, Arranged Marriage, and *Desi* Romance

MALASHRI LAL

The New York Times carries an article called 'The Great Indian Wedding' in which the famous designer Rohit Bal is quoted as saying, 'I had to travel to several cities in Italy and France, to Hong Kong and many other countries to buy the most expensive textiles that I could use for the wedding ensembles.' Bandana Tiwari, author of the article, goes on to say, 'Mr. Bal is happy to traverse the world as he designs and assembles exclusive trousseaus, a selection of 12 to 15 highly customized ensembles that fit into a Louis Vuitton Alzer trunk (for smaller trousseaus) or the Louis Vuitton Malle-Haute (for sizable trousseaus). In India, there is no business like the wedding business.'[11] This 'business' of marriage and all its attendant decisions of ritual and scale are not always made by the brides from these wealthy, privileged backgrounds. There is considerable social pressure and community expectation which drives a bride towards an unquestioning acceptance of parental authority and the opulent show clustered around a 'traditional' wedding. At the other end of the social scale, a

2016 report based on UNICEF documents states that 'India has the highest number of child brides in the world. It is estimated that 47% of girls in India are married before their 18th birthday. In many communities, girls are seen as an economic burden and marriage transfers the responsibility to her new husband. Poverty and marriage expenses such as dowry may lead a family to marry off their daughter at a young age to reduce these costs.'[12] In other words, young women, whether from wealthy or poverty-stricken backgrounds, are not seen as the active players in marriage negotiations or in determining the manner and method of marriage celebrations.

This essay interrogates several assumptions about such powerlessness of women and the claim that India monolithically adopts such a patriarchal stance in denying personal choice or romantic love to the woman in matrimonial contexts. While contemporary goals of conspicuous consumption seem to place much emphasis on the commodities linked to marriage, there appears a counter discourse within history and culture if one were to look for it. Unfortunately, a consumerist global media highlights economic extremes in India and ignores a range of social experiences that constitute everyday lives. From the ancient practice of *Swayamvara* (where the bride reviews a number of suitors and selects one as her husband) to the recent Bollywood film *Queen* of 2014 (where the 'bride' proceeds on a pre-planned honeymoon-vacation by herself after the bridegroom arbitrarily cancels the wedding), there is a long history of critiquing compelled marriages for women. Recognising the diversity of India and its interlinked micro-histories, it would help to recall Mahatma Gandhi's words, 'Man and woman are of equal rank but they are not identical. They are a peerless pair being supplementary to one another; each helps the other, so that without the one the existence of the other cannot be conceived, and therefore it follows as a necessary corollary from these facts that anything that will impair the status of either of them will involve the equal ruin of them both.'[13] Feminist and other critiques of Gandhian frameworks notwithstanding, this, too, is within the Indian tradition.

Swayamvara and the Principle of Woman's Choice

The Sanskrit term '*Swayamvara*' combines two words, '*swayam*' meaning 'self' and '*vara*' meaning 'husband'. India's ancient epics, the *Mahabharata* and *Ramayana*, present significant examples of such selection by the women protagonists of an unfolding epical narrative.

In the context of the *Ramayana*, some years ago, author and festival director Namita Gokhale and I coedited *In Search of Sita: Revisiting Mythology,* in which we dwelt on Sita's strengths and challenged the patriarchal image of Sita as perpetually submissive.[14] Sita's '*swayamvara*' provides one such example. The first *Ramayana*, comprising of 24,000 verses, is said to have been written by Valmiki in the 5th century BC. Sita is found in a furrow by King Janaka, and grows up to demonstrate surprising strength when she, as a young child, casually picks up Shiva's mighty bow with her left hand. In the *swayamvara* organised by King Janaka, Sita is to choose a husband of equal prowess, one who can bend Shiva's bow—and Rama proves to be the only person in the assembly of princes who can accomplish this task. Thereafter the story of kingship, exile, Sita's abduction and the war against Ravana ensues—a story told in many ways across India, that A.K. Ramanujan calls '300 Ramayanas'. The idea of the *swayamvara* is reaffirmed throughout the marital relationship of Rama and Sita, and our book spoke of the recurrent motif of Sita's choice and determination. Reading Valmiki and Tulsidas again carefully, one may notice that Sita asked to accompany Rama to the forest (the royal family wanted her to stay back in the palace), she had the power to keep Ravana away from her in Ashok Vatika while she was his prisoner, she chose to be a single mother to the twins Luv and Kush when abandoned by Rama, and she decided against returning to the kingdom of Ayodhya when Rama discovered his heirs and wanted his queen by his side. Sita's earnest prayers returned her to the womb of mother Earth even as the startled king-husband and his subjects looked on. Therefore, I suggest that the *Swayamvara* denotes not just the moment of matrimonial selection, but a commitment to a renewal and review of that moment throughout life.

The idea of such a choice is not a dated one and, as theorists such as Sudhir Kakar have argued, Sita can be seen to influence self-understandings even today.[15] I had once interviewed Nina Paley about her animated film *Sita Sings the Blues* made in New York. Nina, married to an Indian husband, had been suddenly abandoned by him over an email from India. Perplexed and disturbed, Nina tried to find a cultural understanding of her situation by reading the *Ramayana* in their American home. Here is an excerpt from my interview:

> ML. *Sita Sings the Blues* blurs the distinction between the tragic story of the epic and the comedy of modern lives, especially of women caught in the binds of marital conventions.

> NP. To be clear, *Sita Sings the Blues* isn't a critique of marriage or sexist social conventions: it is an anguished critique of romantic love itself.[16]

So, a further question opens up. Is romantic love compatible with *Swayamvara*? I would say that romantic choice is made in some circumstances but the resultant marriage may not remain romantic. That's a truism about marriages anyway. In the *Mahabharata*, Draupadi's *swayamvara* leads to polyandry, one of the most fascinating aspects of the epic from a feminist viewpoint. Draupadi, born miraculously from a sacred fire, is to marry a person of her choice. The challenge devised at her *swayamvara* is that the suitor must be able to shoot an arrow thorough the eye of a fish revolving on a wheel, which itself is reflected in moving water. At the assembly are only three people capable of fulfilling this daunting task—Krishna, who is only an observer of the event, Karna, adopted son of a low-caste charioteer, and Arjuna, the warrior prince of the Pandavas. Draupadi chooses Arjuna, and insults Karna because of his caste. When Arjuna takes his bride home and calls out to his mother that he has brought a special gift, the mother Kunti says he must share whatever it is with all his brothers. Hence Draupadi becomes the common wife to five husbands. According to the arrangements, she spends one year with each husband exclusively and begets him a child with no confusion about paternity. Before turning to the next husband, Draupadi is said to pass through a purifying fire that turns her into a virgin bride again.

Speaking of *Swayamvara* as an expression of female choice, Draupadi's tale raises complex questions about female sexuality. Her chosen husband is Arjuna but she performs her duty as the wife to each. Further, does she harbour a secret love towards Karna, the handsome warrior she had rejected? This puzzle has been creatively explored by several writers including Mahasweta Devi in the Bengali short story 'Draupadi', Pratibha Ray in the Oriya novel *Yajnaseni* and Chitra Banerjee Divakaruni in her English novel *Palace of Illusions*. Draupadi's sexuality with its public sanction of multiple partners and regulated by a social code, has drawn generations of readers into the discourse on sexual choice or the lack of it. Mahasweta portrays Draupadi as an *adivasi* woman raped by the local police; at the end, Draupadi refuses to hide her mangled body when her clothes are thrown back at her saying, 'What more can you do? Come on *counter* me—come on, *counter* me?'[17]

In all these retellings, the caste issue is foregrounded, bringing Draupadi's story into a contemporary context. Mahasweta Devi's protagonist is from a marginalised community but succeeds in subverting authority by showing up the violence instead of hiding behind a social code of shame. Pratibha Ray and Divakaruni look differently into female power as Draupadi's '*cheer haran*' (pulling away her sari) caused the war of Kurukshetra and transformed history. Traditionally, an Indian woman is said to be protected by her husband, and here even five husbands could not ensure the wellbeing of a shared wife and in fact they perpetrated the disaster. Lord Krishna, the friend or *sakha* to Draupadi, saves her from being publicly disrobed. In other words, Draupadi's choice at the *swayamvara* went wrong—and she is shown to be musing about this in the new readings. Karna, whose royal lineage is hidden from his knowledge and that of others until the eve of the battle of Kurukshetra, may instead have been a more suitable husband for Draupadi.

(In the epic, Karna was born to the royal princess Kunti, an unwed mother seduced by the Sun God. Kunti abandoned the baby, who was then brought up by a low-caste charioteer and his wife). At the core of Draupadi's *swayamvara* episode is thus the tragedy of romantic assumptions in marriage, to be creatively interpreted over centuries.

Literature, Arranged Marriage, and the Denial of Choice

We are not sure when the practice of *Swayamvara* was given up and the process of arranged marriages introduced in ancient India. Often the transition is attributed to the *Manusmriti* (The Laws of Manu), variously dated to be from the 2nd century BCE to the 3rd century CE, which presents itself as a discourse given by Manu and Bhrigu on *dharma* topics such as duties, rights, laws, conduct, virtues and others. This text seems to epitomise patriarchal control over women. In selected verses often cited, the *Manusmriti* preaches that as a girl, she should obey and seek protection of her father, as a young woman her husband, and as a widow her son; and that a woman should always worship her husband as a god. In another set of verses, the *Manusmriti* also declares that 'women must be honoured and adorned', and 'where women are revered, there the gods rejoice; but where they are not, no sacred rite bears any fruit'. Elsewhere, *Manu's Code of Law* declares, according to the translator Patrick Olivelle, that 'a woman must never seek to live independently'[18] even as scholars such as Chandrakala Padia have sought to revisit the *Manusmriti,* reading it through Sanskrit grammar to argue that Manu was not being prescriptive but descriptive about social practice in his times.[19]

For the purpose of this essay, the woman being denied romantic choice is the main issue. Even today, India is associated with arranged marriages, and there seems to be considerable curiosity about the process of finding the 'right match' and how this might extend into a lifelong companionship. To add another interesting layer, it has been claimed that only 1.1 per cent of marriages in India result in a divorce, compared to over 45.8% in the United States.[20]

Literary material on the social phenomenon of arranged marriages is best found in Vikram Seth's novel *A Suitable Boy*, and in Chitra Banerjee Divakaruni's collection of short stories *Arranged Marriage*. As the Punjabi family thought up by Seth describes its priorities, suitability has to be pragmatically described in economic and social terms: caste, class, money, and public position. Post-partition India is the setting for Seth's novel and the intricate confabulations of a Punjabi family over eighteen months provide an entertaining structure. Mrs Rupa Mehra wishes to arrange a 'proper' marriage for her nineteen-year-old college-going daughter Lata, who in her turn refuses to be coerced by her conniving mother and her domineering older brother. The suitors presented are Kabir, Haresh, and Amit, and Lata is to agree to one of them.[21] A massive novel of 1349 pages divided into nineteen sections, the marriage negotiations become the pretext for discussing the emerging politics and debates of the new democracy coming into power. Lata's opposition to her mother is emblematic of the intergenerational struggle and ideological conflicts swarming the nation. In addition, the rise of a new class from previously neglected sections, and the Hindu-Muslim communal divide, tend to influence any personal decisions. Vikram Seth's brilliant epic of post-partition India is built smartly on the trope of an arranged marriage, drawing attention to another form of woman as Mother India and the controls placed over her despite independence. The romance of free choice is denied to the woman, Lata, in this instance, but she is no pushover, and will modify tradition as it suits her.

This flexibility and modernisation of old concepts also frame Chitra Divakaruni's eleven stories in *Arranged Marriage*, many of them about Indians living in America. According to Neelam Mulchandani, 'The women in Divakaruni's texts are caught between the traditional customs of South Asia from which they have emigrated and their present experiences with the more westernized culture of America. While living in such an "in between" space, the self-perceptions of these women are dramatically altered, for the manner in which they see themselves changes due to the uncertain nature of their interstitial environment.'[22] Implicit in such tales is the query as to whether arranged marriages can be happy over time or whether they sour with the realisation that both partners were denied romantic choice. To some extent, the cultural contrast between Indian traditions of marriage and the American freedom of choice plays out in diaspora stories. In many stories, the middle-class immigrant woman struggles with loneliness, professional loss, and the challenge of a new environment. She may overcome this eventually, but the process of such self-discovery is often traumatic. Writings by Bharati Mukherjee, Jhumpa Lahiri and Chitra Banerjee Divakaruni offer many insightful examples of this journey. Looking through the stories in *Arranged Marriage,* one could focus upon 'Meeting Mrinal' as an illustration, a story that is deeply resonant of emotions and richly intertextual. Ashoo, abandoned by her Indian husband and estranged from her young son Dinesh, is beset with despair when she receives a call from her childhood friend, Mrinal, single and successful as a professional. When the two meet, Mrinal seems to envy the 'perfection' of Ashoo's domestic life of marriage and mothering and Ashoo keeps up the pretence of a normative Indian arranged marriage. Returning home, Ashoo imagines the luxury but loneliness of Mrinal's life, but equally recognises the futility of her own. She tries to commit suicide by locking herself in the car, inside the garage and keeping the engine running. Almost faint, she is saved at the last moment with a bitter realisation: 'There's a sweet, heavy smell in the car now. It laps at me, rises past my hips and breasts and mouth to my eyes. And I'm crying—all those tears I didn't shed when Mahesh left, and when Dinesh turned away from me down that harshly lit night corridor. I'm crying for Mrinal in her spacious bed in her luxury apartment, lying alone for the rest of her life, and for myself, who will probably do the same. But most of all I'm crying because I feel like a child who picks up a fairy doll she's always admired from afar and discovers that all its magic and glitter is really painted clay.'

In this narrative, the intertextual reference to Rabindranath Tagore's famous story 'Streer Patra' (The Wife's Letter) should not be missed.[23] In Tagore, the protagonist, Mrinal, writes a letter of farewell to her autocratic husband recounting the many ways in which her identity as a woman was slighted, along with an exposure of patriarchy's oppression of women in general. Refusing to live any more under such coercive authority, Mrinal boldly leaves her 'secure' home for an unspecified destination. In Chitra Divakaruni's story, Mrinal is a version of this free woman. Furthermore, Banerjee's protagonist Ashoo bemoans her perceived inadequacy in terms of expected social norms in India: 'I think of how hard I always tried to be the perfect wife and mother, like the heroines of mythology I grew up on—patient, faithful Sita, selfless Kunti'. Here too the intertextual irony with the Hindu epics is intended. Sita was faithful to Rama but that did not ensure marital happiness, and Kunti—who had abandoned Karna, and willed Draupadi to be shared by her five sons—could hardly be praised for being selfless. Divakaruni has a wise saying in *The Palace of Illusions*, her novel about Draupadi: 'Love comes like lightning, and disappears the same way. If you are lucky, it strikes you right. If not, you'll spend your life yearning for a man you can't have.'[24]

Bollywood Dreams

The mystique of true love is the stuff of dreams—whether it is approached through a self-choosing tradition akin to *Swayamvara* or to parental selection determining arranged marriages. (Incidentally, there is no Hindi equivalent of the term 'arranged marriage.') It is no wonder, then, that Bollywood, that purveyor of social mapping in India, finds marriage to be a favourite subject for multiple levels of exploration.

The first film to play upon the specific word was *Swayamvar* (1980), directed by P. Sambasiva Rao and with a star cast including Sanjeev Kumar and Shashi Kapoor in character roles called Ram and Laxman. Predictably, their function was to destroy evil, which is the imperious Durgadevi (Nadira) and others standing in the way of true love.

Though one must jump two decades, it's worth noting

that the film *Monsoon Wedding* (2002) is the ultimate visual narrative of a complex arranged marriage in India in which 'the family' is more important than the couple being married. Lalit Verma (Naseeruddin Shah) and his wife Pimmi (Lillete Dubey) have arranged a marriage for their daughter Aditi (Vasundhara Das) to Hemant Rai (Parvin Dabas). Director Meera Nair's great success is in depicting a post-partition Punjabi clan in Delhi going through magnificent wedding preparations that inadvertently expose hidden secrets and psychological vulnerabilities in several characters. Social issues such as gender and sexuality, economic concerns such as loans and subsidies against a backdrop of globalization, and class discrimination such as the exploitation of domestic workers, all find their place in this intricate plot. The wedding is the stage on which an elaborate performance is mounted by both the families—the groom's family from the USA and the bride's from Delhi, but aided financially by relatives from abroad. The couple, Hemant and Aditi, have barely met, but confessions of past affairs tumble out, are forgiven and kissed away—and the monsoon rains cascade over the large happy Indian family enjoying a big fat Indian wedding. In an interview published in *The Guardian*, Meera Nair said *Monsoon Wedding* was 'a love song to my home city'. Delhi is a city of excess and contrasts. Nair elaborated, 'It was important for me to show along with the upper middle-class—which is my own upbringing—the life of the working class. It's terrible and true that we have thousands of people just serving us and they all have a world, they all have a life, they all have a story.'[25]

Bollywood continued to work on middle class sentiments spreading the good feeling—hugging the dream of perfect arranged marriages in films such as Sooraj R. Barjatya's musical comedy *Hum Aapke Hain Koun!* (1994), Sanjay Leela Bhansali's sentimental sojourn *Hum Dil De Chuke Sanam* (1999) and Vipul Amrutlal Shah's international travelogue *Namastey London* (2007). The philosophy is to convince the audience that romance may come after marriage, not necessarily always before—and that arranged marriages, where compatibility is checked out by wiser and older people, may sometimes promise a better chance of life-long happiness than a spontaneous overflow of powerful feelings between heady youngsters. The institution of matchmakers, astrologers, horoscope readers, matrimonial advertising, wedding planners and such others thus become aspects of a lucrative industry.

This bubble of engineered happiness was, of course, bound to burst, even in the entertainment industry, at a time when domestic violence, street crime against women and acts of sexual harassment at the workplace showed women in India in more realistic circumstances. Bollywood responded with its own re-make of the dream of happiness. The film *Queen* (2014), written and directed by Vikas Bahl, is outstanding in its depiction of the new woman who is neither married nor unmarried, but precariously poised at the cusp of both conditions. The film debunks arranged marriages and patriarchy through humour and social satire. Kangana Ranaut's acting as the small-town girl Rani Mehra who evolves into a cosmopolitan person drives home the message that marriage is ultimately unimportant to personal happiness. The plot shows the bridegroom Vijay walking out of the arranged marriage one day before the wedding ceremony, claiming that his exposure to London had made his chosen bride Rani unsuitable for his new lifestyle. Rani, insulted and heartbroken, nevertheless rallies around and convinces her parents that she will proceed to Amsterdam and Paris on the pre-planned honeymoon itinerary, without a husband! Taking on the travel with curiosity and increasing self-confidence, Rani figures out her way through hotels, nightclubs, a backpackers' den, and even sex shops. Her innate intelligence and warmth brings friends into her life—those who know Europe and wish her to succeed. Vijay now finds her an attractive companion and imagines that the old arranged marriage terms can be revived, but Rani wants no more of this. The last scene in Delhi, when Rani returns her engagement ring to Vijay with a 'thank you' note and a smile, is the final endorsement of feminist freedom from patriarchal impositions.

Along with *Queen,* Bollywood has offered a few other powerful women-centric movies such as *Dirty Picture, Kahaani, Mary Kom* and *Mardani* showing the way to feminist selfhood in the current decade. However, the romanticised family sagas continue, albeit disguised as mythology or history and offering visual spectacle on the grandest scale. *Bajirao Mastani* (2015) and *Baahubali 2: The Conclusion* (2017) would fall into this category.

In summary, romantic love and female sexuality are subjects openly discussed in Indian literature and cinema now, far more than before. In a recent book *Incarnations: A History of India in Fifty Lives* (2016), which covers 2500 years of history, Sunil Khilnani, director of the India Institute at King's College London, writes, 'Indian history is a curiously unpeopled place...As usually told, it has dynasties, epochs, religions and castes—but not many individuals.'[26] He corrects the omissions in some ways by refusing to write linear narratives, and creating biographical sketches of people who impacted history—famous ones such as Buddha and Gandhi but also the lesser known ones such as Malik Ambar, 17th century guerrilla leader, and Birsa Munda, a tribal activist under colonialism. But the domestic domain of love and loss hardly figures on such a national canvas, and Khilnani's poignant sketch of the Indian-Hungarian artist Amrita Sher Gill makes the point about rebel identity in women having to first contend against normative notions of family and community. In such a context it is a useful reminder that India moves in simultaneous time zones, the living mythology of the *Ramayana* and *Mahabharata* influencing modern lives as much as mobile phones and Netflix. With this simultaneity, 'arranged marriages' as well as 'love marriages', family sagas as well as individual rebellions will carry on as intrinsic components of India's vibrancy. So long as literature and cinema provide internal critiques, a healthy matrix is assured.

Radha, Divine Paramour

MAKARAND R. PARANJAPE

Sri Radha, Lord Krishna's soul mate and paramour, is a unique phenomenon in the religious and spiritual history not just of India but of the world, a humble milkmaid elevated to the supreme status of the erotic as well as holy beloved of the Supreme Godhead.[27] Given her unique position in the Hindu imaginary, what would Radharani say to Mahatma Gandhi if he were suddenly to encounter her in the vast landscapes of Hindu thought as he tried to purify and rid himself of all carnal desires? An answer to such a question—conjectural, philosophical and provocative—as posed by this essay may well be our unexpected reward as we try to understand the importance of being Radha.[28]

The rise of Radha coincides with the widest popularity of Vaishnavism, especially the post-Chaitanya ecstatic mode of Krishna-bhakti. The male-dominated theology of Vaishnavism before Radha suffered from a particularly acute Goddess-deficit. The first three avatars, *matsya, kurma, varaha*, are sub-human; Vaman is single and short; Narasimha, half-man, half-lion, though later paired with Lakshmi, has no real relationship with her. With Rama we see the beginning of a real love story. The romance of Sita-Rama is indeed charming, especially their first meeting resulting in the *svayamvara*, and their enchanting honeymoon in Chitrakoot. But Sita's subsequent humiliations, her trial by fire and, finally, her banishment when pregnant, turns the love story into a tragedy. That is why not just the Vaishnava revival but even feminine-dominant Shaktism needed the special kind of love-Goddess that Radha became. In the process, she also made Krishna the most attractive and irresistible of the avatars. Radha has the kind of agency and independence that Lakshmi or the other consorts of Vishnu lack. Even if she is shown often as subservient to Krishna, her life history, as scholars such as Jessica Frazier have argued, can be read as demonstrating extraordinary female agency and empowerment. [29]

What makes Radha's story unique is that she is hardly mentioned in the classical sources or scriptures. Even later, during the medieval period after the 12th century CE, while the name of Radha is in wider circulation, her rise to prominence as an important Goddess alongside Krishna is actually a comparatively recent phenomenon. According to Charlotte Vaudeville, 'her emergence in the cultic and devotional sphere of Vaishnavism as Krishna Gopala's beloved and *sakti* is known to have taken place rather late, certainly not much earlier than the sixteenth century'.[30]

In the Bhagavata Purana (8th to 10th century CE), the source of much of the later Krishna cult, there is no reference to Radha. The only clue to her identity is the mention of the single, unnamed girl with whom Krishna disappears in the Tenth Canto, which celebrates Krishna's amours in the forest on the night of the full moon. While all the *gopis* cavort with Krishna in that scene, there is one he takes aside, much to the consternation, even despair, of the others. Perhaps, that exceptional partner gave our medieval myth-makers the germ of the story of Radha which Jayadeva narrates in *Gitagovinda*. As Guy L. Beck notes:

> Within the entire Sanskrit canon that is accepted by normative Vaishnava traditions, Radha is actually never mentioned by name. In the earlier canonical texts there is only the suggestion of Radha's character, not her actual name, as one of Krishna's favorites among a number of 'unmarried' (*Harivamsa*) or 'already married' (*Bhagavata Purana*) cowherd girls (gopis) who nonetheless seek his attentions during his childhood life in Braj.[31]

The prehistory of Radha, thus, at best remains elusive. In the most detailed and painstaking study of her origins, Jayadeva's translator Barbara Stoler Miller points out that prior to Jayadeva there are very few references to Radha:

> The figure of Radha is one of the most elusive in Sanskrit literature. Until Jayadeva made her the heroine of his poem, she appeared only in stray verses scattered through anthologies of Prakrit and Sanskrit poetry, works of literary aesthetics, grammar, poetry, and drama, and a few inscriptions.[32]

But this does not mean that she was completely unknown earlier. Miller documents the several stray references to her in Puranic and literary texts, suggesting that the idea of the 'awesome' love couple, Radha-Krishna, was already 'established and widespread by late classical times': Radha was the 'special gopi whose secret love with Krsna is enacted in a thicket on the Jamna riverbank deep in Vrndavana forest.'[33] In a fascinating speculation using etymological and astral references, Miller conjectures: The name Radha thus came to carry overtones of meaning from both its etymology and 'astral mythology.' The somewhat 'esoteric' character of these associations may have increased the appeal of Radha as a consort for Krsna in a secret, erotic relationship.[34]

One of the sources of Radha is the Tamil beauty, Nappinnai, who in the compositions of the Alvar poets Nammalvar and Andal, is Krishna's wife and the daughter (or daughter-in-law) of Nandagopal. However, following Vaudeville's lead in 'Evolution of Love-Symbolism in Bhagavatism'[35], Miller rejects this idea, arguing instead that the two are quite different, especially in their emphasis: 'It is possible that Nappinnai is the source of the Radha conception in Prakrit and Sanskrit literature, but the two figures more likely represent independent variants; their characteristics are different.'[36] The antecedents of Jayadeva's Radha, thus, remain 'one of the puzzles of Sanskrit literature.'[37]

Though the references to Radha before Jayadeva are so sketchy, Kinsley believes that the main aspects of her character, however, are already encapsulated in them.[38] Radha is 'a lovesick girl or woman', emotionally volatile, 'angered while making love to Krishna' and 'leaving him while choking on her tears' in *Venisamhara* of Bhatta Narayana (before CE 800).[39] In Abhinavagupta's *Dhvanyalokalocana* (early tenth century), Radha is shown weeping inconsolably when Krishna leaves Vrindavan.[40] Ksemendra's *Dasavataracarita* depicts her as speechless with sorrow, but nevertheless highly eroticized, 'With tears, flowing away like life in Madhava's desertion/Falling on her breasts' firm tips'; she is compared with 'the laden *kadamba* tree', blinded by her tears, endlessly sighing and trembling, her 'gait/ Darkened by the delusion that was bound to all her hopes', she becomes 'like the new rainy season engulfed in darkness'.[41] These portrayals are dominated by *viraha* or love in separation.

Thus it is to Jayadeva and his remarkable *Gitagovinda* that the real credit for developing fully the complex character of Radha goes. As Valerie Ritter says:

> The *Gitagovinda,* a highly popular and influential Sanskrit poem by Jayadeva, thought to have been composed in the twelfth to thirteenth centuries CE, was the first to focus extensively on Radha, in a manner evocative of the courtly *nayaka* and *nayika* (hero and heroine) of Sanskrit poetry.[42]
>
> But when Jayadeva makes her a full-fledged *nayika* or heroine of his most influential poem, *Gitagovinda*, it seems as if we have always 'known' or at least craved for Radha's presence, nay, predominance in the love story of Krishna.[43]

Once created by Jayadeva, Radha steadily rises in importance as Krishna's chosen paramour, partner, spouse (as she was later in the Radhavallabha sect), and thus the supreme Vaishnava Goddess. Chaitanya Mahaprabhu (1486–1534), who gave the Krishna cult its decisive form, at least in much of northern and eastern India, contributed a great deal to the theology if not character of Radha. As Beck points out:

> Radha's presence in poetry and her theological importance increased with the growth of the Caitanyite sect of Vaishnavism in Bengal, which saw the integration of poetic theory of the *sringara rasa* (the erotic sentiment) and its taxonomies of the *nayaka-nayika* with theology concerning the love of Radha and Krishna.[44]

While the *Gitagovinda* institutionalized and legitimated Radha's centrality in Vaishnavite *bhakti* literature, her character, persona, and role was further embellished and moulded by eastern Indian poets like Chandidas and Vidyapati, who created the platform for the great devotional and political upsurge marked by the advent of Chaitanya. Others, notably Nimbarka who was closer to Jayadeva, and Vallabha (around the same time as Chaitanya), also played a crucial role.[45] Later, most of the great Krishna-worshipping poets such as Surdas also adored Radha till she became his secularized and universalized erotic partner in the Riti Kala poets like Bihari (1595-1664).

With the beginnings of colonial modernity in India, Radha the Goddess underwent another drastic modification, now coming more often than not to represent illegitimate sexual desire. In the new puritanism fostered during the so-called Indian renaissance (eighteenth to nineteenth centuries), Radha and her dalliance with Krishna proved an embarrassment to the agenda of social reform that the proponents of Hindu respectability espoused. Yet, Radha persisted in folk songs and, later, in many popular art and craft traditions. The final twist in the Radha tale was added by twentieth century representations, by feminists who began to see in her a victim of patriarchy or even by male writers as their special symbol and voice, as in Ramakant Rath's celebrated *Sri Radha*.[46] Sometimes, Radha became a symbol of the degraded and exploited woman, even a fallen or abandoned woman, her tale a cautionary reminder of what happens to such women in our society.

All told, the story of Radha is extraordinary, not only in itself, but in the larger context of the history of Indian art, culture, religion, and spirituality. The reasons for the rise of Radha are not merely historical, but theological, metaphysical, and spiritual too. If such a methodology has explanatory power, then it may also account for the decline of Radha.

Let us now glance, briefly, at Radha in all her glory in the middle of the sixteenth century. By now, Jayadeva's *Gitagovinda* has been in circulation for nearly four hundred years. Nimbarka and Vallabha have already accepted, even celebrated her, in their own compositions and in the theology of their *sampradaya*s. But it is Chaitanya who really establishes the centrality of Radha in the worship of Krishna. As Graham M. Schewig observes:

> The divine couple, Radha and Krishna, comprise the essence of the godhead. Radha is therefore acknowledged by Chaitanyaite Vaishnavas to be part of the very center of their theological doctrine, as reflected in their liturgical practices. Sacred images of the forms of Radha and Krishna, standing together side by side, are elaborately worshiped in Indian temples.[47]

Chaitanya accomplished this by personally experiencing and exalting 'Radha *bhava*', the state of being Radha-like, which gave the cult of Radha its biggest boost. Now Radha becomes not just one of the gopis or even Krishna's chosen partner, but, indeed, the symbol of the perfect beloved and the preferred way of reaching or obtaining Krishna. Wherever Radha is, Krishna also abides; therefore every devotee must not only pay obeisance to her but, in being Radha-like, attract the attention of Krishna, indeed, even *enjoy* Krishna as Radha herself did. So important did Radha become that Krishna was sometimes given second place, assumed to be implicit to adoration of Radha; a practice that still persists till date. Several of Chaitanya's followers also extolled her virtues, celebrating her as Krishna's perfect lover and partner.

The general regard for Radha during this period became so high that even an otherwise 'secular' and largely erotic cycle of poems such as Bihari's *Satsai* of seven hundred couplets reflects this, as demonstrated by the opening *doha* (distich):

> *meri bhavabaadhaa harau radha naagari soi*
> *jaa tan ki jhaaim paraim syaama harit duti hoi.*

The *Satsai* of Bihari is arguably the most celebrated Hindi poem of what is called the Riti Kaal or the age of courtly poetry.[48] One index of its importance is that it has more than seventeen commentaries and was translated into Sanskrit twice. It was also illustrated extensively, especially by the Kangra painters, and its verses set to music. It thus came to occupy a central position in the literary and cultural life of northern India of the seventeenth century. That the opening *doha* is also used as a *mangalacaran* or an auspicious invocatory verse is quite significant. The placement of Radha in the invocatory opening verse of one of the most important poems of the period signifies that her apotheosis was by then complete. Radha by the early seventeenth century is therefore a full-fledged Goddess, the principal and chosen deity not just of the Vaishnavite devotees of Krishna, but also of the leading courtly poet of the time.

The meaning of the couplet is by no means simple. It is, on the contrary, complex, allusive, and multi-layered, thus making it difficult to render into English. The flattened and simplistic translations prevalent scarcely do it justice, as several key words in the couplet can be translated in at least three different ways according to their various meanings: for example, *shyama* (black, Krishna, or blackness as taint) or *harit duti* (green lustre, removed brightness, or lost property).[49] In what follows I try to convey the meaning of the couplet:

> May that skilled Radha take away the suffering of my existence,
> By the shadow of whose body Shyam turns lustrous green.

Or:

> She who removes my existential distress is artful Radha
> By the glimpse of whose body Shyama's darkness become lustrous green.

'Lustrous green' is one of the possible translations of '*harit duti*'. The second line of the couplet could also mean that the very shadow of Radha's body turns Krishna from black into luminous green; steals Krishna's lustre; or removes the stain (of sin). The second meaning is somewhat hard to comprehend: why should Radha's very shadow steal Krishna's lustre? What is suggested is that Krishna is so overpowered by his attraction to Radha that even the shadow of her body can make him lose his self-possession or shine. In any case, the *doha* asserts the power, even supremacy of Radha, not only in her ability to overcome Krishna, changing his colour or taking away his brightness, or removing the stain of sin, but also in saving the poet himself by eradicating the latter's *bhava baadhaa*, pecuniary, if not existential, distress. If it is admitted that all of us suffer from some version or the other of the latter, then

Radha as saviour or redeemer is indeed a very attractive figure.

The colour symbolism in the couplet is impossible to ignore: when yellow and blue are mixed, the outcome is green. Krishna is *shyama* or blue-black, while Radha is golden yellow in hue; their mixture leads, literally, to the greening of Krishna, a vernal deity if there was one, representing pastoral perfection. Clearly, in this context, Krishna is not green with envy, an emotion seldom associated with him, but with love, his characteristic mode of being, but in this instance, derived from Radha. What, however, might the theological implications of this colour chemistry be? Colouring and dyeing are prevalent metaphors for spiritual transformation throughout medieval poetry. Falling in love and being united with one's beloved is often spoken of as being dyed in the latter's colours (hence the title of Mishra's book, *Radha Madhava Rang Rangi*—'Radha coloured in Krishna's hue').[50] When the devotee surrenders totally to the deity, she becomes imbued with the latter's complexion. But in this case, it is Radha who gives her colour to Krishna, again emphasizing her importance in his lifework. Krishna's greening or blossoming is effected by Radha's love for him. It is she who steals his native lustre only to replenish it with her own effulgence. It is Radha who is responsible for the flowering of Krishna; she makes him fertile and fecund, turning him into the 'evergreen' love God, thus amplifying his power and glory as none other could.

I have translated '*naagari*', Bihari's unusual epithet for Radha, as skilled or artful in preference to Bahadur's 'gifted'.[51] Bihari, the courtly poet, constructs Radha as Krishna's sophisticated, skilful, *urban*, match rather than a guileless, naive milkmaid of Vrindavan, the epitome of pastoral innocence and beauty. Radha, by the time she becomes the fully developed protagonist of the *Rasakrida* or the love-play of the dark God, acquires a somewhat dual significance as being both artless and sophisticated all at once. As Valerie Ritter observes, 'In Braj-dialect Hindi literature (as well as other languages), Radha continued her double life as both a simple gopi and a sophisticated lover (*naagari*) of Krishna, in poetry comprised of both popular devotional lyrics and courtly poetry.'[52] No wonder Bihari, more courtly than devotional, crafts his Radha as artful not only in dalliance and love, but also adroit in saving souls such as his from the distress of worldly existence (*bhava baadha*). Radha's high status is also amply illustrated in other texts of the period, especially Surdas's famous *Sursagar.*

This elevated status of Radha persists to this day in the area around Vrindavan, the legendary site of young Krishna's amorous dalliance with the *gopis* or 'cow girls'. These simple women become the embodiments of the highest spiritual attainment and symbols of supreme devotion to the Godhead, giving rise to India's own pastoral paradise, an Edenic, unfallen world in which eros is not tainted by lust, and God himself frolics with his devotees in never-ending moonlit nights of ecstasy in the charmed forest clearing. Here Radha, as Krishna's love-interest, indeed rules. Even the normal greeting of common people in this area to this day is 'Radhe Radhe'. For her worshippers, then, Radha is indeed the supreme source of delight or *ananda*; she literally rains down rasa, or relish, times manifold than even Krishna:

brahmananda-rasad ananta-gunito ramyo raso vaisnavas
tasmat koti-gunojjvalas ca madhurah sri-gokulendro rasah

tac cananta-camatkatim pratimuhur varsad rasanam param
sri-radha-pada-padmam eva madhuram sarvasva-bhutam mama

> Countless times more relishable than the flavour of Brahmananda is that connected to Vishnu. Millions of times brighter than that is the sweet rasa related to the Lord of Gokula. Raining down infinite astonishment are the topmost of all rasas, the sweet lotus feet of Srimati Radharani. They alone are my life and soul.[53]

The rise of Radha was facilitated by the widely prevalent Shakta cults in medieval India as Radha, 'aligned and identified' with Bhagavati or the Supreme Goddess attained a status higher even than Krishna.[54] For example, in the *Devi-Bhagavata Purana*, Narayana is shown to worship Radha:

> Salutations to the supreme goddess, who resides at *Rasamandala,* who lords over the *Rasa* and is dearer to Krishna than his own life. Salutation to the mother of all the three worlds, whose lotus-like feet are worshipped by gods headed by Brahma and Visnu. Be propitiated, Oh, Ocean of mercy.[55]

Mother of three worlds, worshipped by all the male Gods—these are typical descriptions of the Mother Goddess, applied clearly to Radha, identified as the mistress of the *Rasamandala*. Radha as Bhagavati is a Shakta appropriation just as Radha as Lakshmi (Sri, Kamala, Padma, and so on) was the more conventional Vaishnava adaptation.

The *Brahmavaivarta Purana* goes even farther. Like the *Devi-Bhagavata*, this *Purana* was also composed in Bengal, where Tantrism and Vaishnavism freely intermingled. Krishna calls Radha his support: he 'rests eternally' upon her; without her he would not exist.[56] As in Shakta traditions, she, on the other hand is *svadhina,* supreme and self-sufficient, needing no other *adhar* (prop). Radha as the supreme power animates Krishna; without her he is inert, as Shiva is without Shakti. Radha is also identified with the Mother of the world, while Krishna is the father; as is to be expected in a Shakta text, 'the mother, however, is declared to be the guru of the father and as such is said to be worshiped as supreme.'[57] Kinsley concludes, 'Radha's elevated status, her role as cosmic queen equal to or superior to Krsna, gives her a central role in the cosmogony in the *Brahma-vaivarta-purana*.'[58] This exaltation of Radha to a status above even Krishna is in keeping with Tantric traditions of the worship of the Supreme Mother. But it also adds a new dimension to Radha. In the prior or later literature, she is never seen as a mother, but primarily as a young woman, and lover, even when she is someone else's wife. In the *Brahmavaivarta Purana*, in contrast, she is invested with several motherly epithets including Mahavishnormatri and Mahavishudhatri (mother of Vishnu), Jaganmatri and Jagadambika (mother of the world), and Sarvamatri (mother of all.)[59]

Paradoxically, the same text that exalts her to a status higher than Krishna himself, also depicts her as a 'chaste and jealous wife,' extremely possessive of Krishna, 'outraged, jealous, and vengeful' when it comes to his other dalliances.[60] Her rage fits terrify even Krishna; as to her other rivals, one, Viraja, even prefers suicide to facing her wrath, Kinsley contending that this 'cruel, selfish, and demanding' Radha is no longer as charming as the 'lovelorn, innocent milkmaid of Braja.'[61] But, surely, Krishna's appeasement and flattery of Radha is not entirely new; it is quite well-developed even in the *Gitagovinda*. The Tantric Radha, who is independent and superior to Krishna, is thus quite expectedly shown as behaving as though she 'owns' Krishna. The rage of the Mother Goddess is a throwback to an earlier time of untamed Goddesses and Yoginis who unleashed terror and mayhem when they were crossed. These wild and untamed deities were later domesticated and incorporated into the *Rasamandala*, which represents a stable and ordered containment of desire, with Krishna at its centre. In the eternal battle of the sexes, carried out even at the divine level, the Goddess has her due here, while she is disciplined elsewhere.

If anything, the Tantric Radha is even more awesome than the Pauranic. The *Kalivilasa Tantra,* for instance, an eastern Indian text, composed like the above-mentioned *Puranas* in Bengal or Assam, has a section on Radha.[62] Here, as might be expected of a Shakta text, Krishna is the son of the Devi, who was Gauri (the fair one) before she turned dark with passion. Krishna, by suckling the Mother Goddess, becomes Saguna (with qualities and attributes) from his original Nirguna (quality- and attribute-less) state. Chapter XXVIII also talks of Radha's union with Krishna.[63]

If Radha is mentioned in passing in such texts, there is in fact an entire *Tantra* devoted to her, though it is somewhat obscure and seldom discussed. The *Radha Tantra*, according to Banerji, is 'an anonymous work of unknown date and provenance'[64] composed and available in Bengal, with most of its extant manuscripts written in Bangla letters. Again, Krishna is the son of Tripura Sundari, the Supreme Goddess. She initiates him to the Kulachara, which Krishna follows with Padmini or Radha, who is one of the manifestations of the Goddess herself. Again, we see here a fusion of Shaktism and Vaishnavism.

To return to the opening verses from *Satsai*, it is easy to see how they mark the transformation of Radha from *gopi* to Goddess, consequent upon the consolidation of her cult. Radha thus becomes Krishna's fittest spouse in the new Krishnology. But how and why did such a radical apotheosis take place? And what might its metaphysical and spiritual significance be? Radha, it would seem, is largely a medieval phenomenon. She doesn't exist in the classical world nor does she quite survive as a Goddess in the harsh dawn of modernity.

From the late classical to the medieval period, we notice a fundamental shift from the Advaitic orthodoxy of Sankara to the qualified non-dualism, theism, and Vaishnavism of other *acharyas* or founders of lineages such as Ramanuja, Madhva, Nimbarka, and Vishnuswami. Some of these schools built up a considerable devotional literature around Krishna in both Sanskrit and the vernaculars, with Krishna as the favoured avatar of Vishnu. But the rise of Radha was propelled by newer and smaller groups who went even farther, considering Krishna not just as the favourite avatar of Vishnu, but as the supreme Godhead, the only being worthy of worship, one who embodied all the divine perfection and grace in himself. As Beck explains:

> Between 1500–1600 CE, a number of newer but smaller Vaishnava *sampradayas* were founded or modified from previous *sampradayas* in the late medieval or Mughal period in which the status of Krishna was elevated further. These new movements generally favored Krishna as the Supreme Being, over and above Vishnu, and drew even more exclusively on vernacular poetry from within their respective traditions that exalted Krishna's childhood pastimes.[65]

It was extraordinary how these groups established themselves around Braj, between Delhi and Agra, believing after Chaitanya, that this was indeed the lost or forgotten site of the frolics of Krishna's boyhood.

Thus they imagined into being a new pastoral geography for the conquered Hindus in the very heart of the Mughal power, a feat that must have involved considerable political skill and economic ingenuity in addition to unprecedented devotional fervour. The legend of Vrindavan was thus born for which, I would argue, the figure of Radha was the key ingredient. As the cult of Radha grew, these new Vaishnavite traditions converted Radha's illicit or adulterous relationship with Krishna to a higher theological principle of the indivisibility of God's masculine and feminine aspects or of the soul's inseparability from God. Whatever the ruse, it was Radha that was worshipped alongside Krishna in innumerable temples, not one of his legally wedded wives. The exception to this is Rukmini, who is given pride of place in the Vitthal cult in Maharashtra, where it is Vitthal-Rakumai, not Radha-Krishna that forms the Divine pair. But even in the Vitthal *sampradaya*, the Devi's temple is usually separate from the Lord's; they are rarely conjoint as in the Radha-Krishna coupling. Thus over time, the more disturbing or heterodox aspects of the Radha-Krishna story were smoothened out. Yet, the slightly uneasy and transgressive dimension of the relationship could not be altogether banished. As Beck observes:

> The relation between Radha as 'favorite' and Krishna is a tentative one of lover and paramour, not of husband and wife. In the vernacular Bengali poems of Chandidas, for example, Radha is already married to someone named Ayana, and in Bengali *kirtan* singing that name is

> completed as Ayana Ghosh. In the Sanskrit plays of Rupa Goswamin, Radha is already married to Abhimanyu, heightening the intensity of their illicit connection.[66]

Later, when the disassociation of sensibility, so to speak, between the erotic and the sacred, was completed in nineteenth-century Bengal, the Radha-Krishna relationship outside the Gaudiya *parampara* began to be used more often in a ribald and prurient sense, even to encourage or camouflage what the *bhadralok* or gentle folk considered licentious or improper conduct.

But from the thirteenth to the seventeenth centuries, what the Radha-Krishna coupling represented was love that was simultaneously intensely erotic and devotional. We would be mistaken, as Lee Siegel reminds us, to see the Radha-Krishna pairing in purely symbolic or allegorical terms, at least in a text like *Gitagovinda*:

> The *Gitagovinda* is not so much an allegorical work as an allegorically interpreted work... [T]he *Gitagovinda* is literally about carnal love but it is also literally devotional. There was no contradiction...The need to read the poem allegorically, to interpret the sexuality as a mere analogy for the spiritual relationship, wholly differentiated from it, arises only when celibacy is idealized, when sexuality becomes a transgression against religions ideals.[67]

The predominantly allegorical interpretations thus came afterwards, as a way to hide or rationalize what later generations saw as unacceptable or impure, after sexuality began to be met with disapproval and repression. During its heyday, the Radha-Krishna relationship embodied a sex-positive mystical cult in which sexual fulfilment was very much a part of self-realization. After the colonial intervention, Indian spiritual traditions took a decisive turn towards celibacy, from which we have not yet recovered fully, despite the silent but rather obvious sexual revolution that has overpowered India in recent decades. Nearly every notable spiritual guru or leader including Sri Swami Narayan, Sri Ramakrishna, Swami Vivekananda, Mahatma Gandhi, Sri Aurobindo, Ramana Maharshi, J. Krishnamurti, Swami Sivananda, Satya Sai Baba, and so on has been an open advocate, or largely in favour, of sexual abstinence for serious spiritual practitioners. Some have been silent or hypocritical, saying one thing but found out practicing another. Only Osho (Rajneesh) was openly contemptuous of the celibacy-fetish; indeed, there is an impression, probably mistaken, that he encouraged sex as a way to superconsciousness. Of course, his followers, even those who took 'sanyas' or vowed renunciation, were not called upon to give up sex.

Thus Radha in her heyday not only defies the whore vs. virgin mother dichotomy that has plagued most cultures of the world in their fear and exaltation of female sexuality, but she has managed to embody an unfallen eros, so rare in romantic traditions anywhere. Unlike other famous love stories, the Radha-Krishna myth is not about the impossibility of perfect love on earth, but rather its fullest expression and celebration.

It is, however, another matter that Krishna must leave the *gopis*. In the story as canonized in the *Bhagavata Purana*, the *gopis* of Brindavan have higher wisdom and status than *jnanis* or knowers of *advaita* (non-dualism) because despite physical separation, they continuously experience Krishna in their hearts and are therefore ever united with him. But unlike Catholic nuns, who are also supposed to be brides of Christ, the *gopis have* experienced physical union with Krishna, dancing in ecstasy with him in the heart of the forest on that special full moon night that lasted for a thousand years when Krishna united with each one of them physically. The thus ravished *gopis* have forever learned the impossibly difficult lesson of undying union, a wisdom perhaps higher than all other paths to know God. The story of Radha and Krishna, at least in the *Gitagovinda,* is one of found-lost-and-found love, not of found-and-lost or even lost-and-found love:

> Union-separation-reunion, is the conventional pattern in Indian erotic literature. But it is also the archetypal structure in Indian ontology... For the individual liberation is reunion, a return to the primordial unity, a recovery of the unborn Self.[68]

Hence, the *Gitagovinda* ends with the supreme joy of oneness and physical rapture, not with tearful separation or sorrow, which would necessitate a deferral of ecstasy with the promise of eternal union in the hereafter. In contrast, fulfilment of earthly love is impossible in the here and now for many other traditions, given their other-worldly eschatology, but must always be postponed to the hereafter; when it comes to complete gratification, most romantic traditions offer no immediate encashment, but only post-dated, largely posthumous cheques to thwarted lovers.

This is what happens, for instance, in *Romeo and Juliet* or *Anarkali*, to name two different but equally powerful takes on romantic love. Even in representations in Islam of Sufi romantic love, the last or ultimate stage is *fana* or death, often interpreted as the death of the separate self, but usually depicted in physical fatality at the end of the story, whether in the legend of Laila-Majnu, Shirin-Farhad, or Heer-Ranjha. It is only in the Persian story of Yusuf-Zulekha that the lovers enjoy earthly fulfilment after all their trials, but that too because the unique and unprecedented transfiguration of Zulekha, who represents the earth-bound soul, happens on earth itself, when her youth and beauty are restored by God because of Yusuf's good offices. The story stresses her exceptional fortune because ordinarily such a transformation could only be possible in heaven, after her death. The traditional pattern in Christian love stories is also 'the separation of lovers, both temporarily and through various obstructions and permanently through death.'[69]

The Radha-Krishna story, unlike all these, takes place on earth, in the enchanted space of Vrindavan, in a peculiarly bold and unprecedented pastoral setting in India, in a world that is not prelapsarian, but radically unfallen, even infallible, because of the power and glory of the supreme Godhead sporting with his creation as the Purushottama, the perfected human form. What has been effected is a reversal of the Platonic schema, with the idea(l) instantiated here and now, right in our midst, though in sacred and mythical time, while even the heavens, ordinarily endowed with unearthly perfection and immortality, end up looking pale and second-best in comparison. The pastoral God-child, Krishna, defies and defeats Indra, the King of Heaven, thus upturning the Vedic cosmology and hierophany. Earth is now superior to heaven; Krishna, or Vishnu in his perfect human embodiment, is superior to the Gods in their heaven; the provisional delusion of separation which allows us to enjoy God is superior to non-dualistic monism, which is not only monochrome but apparently lacking in *rasa* or relish.

Radha-Krishna shows us God as an object of

sensual enjoyment in a way that such an experience at once turns supra-sensual, defying the normal structure of human corporeal experiences. What we see is neither an assertion of the supremacy of sense experience as the logic positivists might uphold, nor the valorization of God as the transcendental signified, above and beyond all sense data. Instead, it is intense, pure-hearted, and transformative love that came to be concentrated in the single unique person of Radha. Unlike the shame of Adam and Eve on eating the fruit of the tree of knowledge, discovering their nakedness and covering themselves when they appeared before God, the *gopis* bathing in the lake, though full of shame, consciously, deliberately, and lovingly emerge from the lake to be utterly nude before God, thus not only losing their shame, but gaining dignity and self-realization through such exposure to the Divine gaze. Their love makes them pure and innocent, quite unlike the 'fallen' Adam and Eve. It is not a case of innocence lost, but rather of innocence regained. Loving surrender to God gives us back our pristine purity instead of making us fallen in our own eyes. The male gaze, in this case Krishna's, is not prurient, objectifying, or oppressive, but elevating, innocence-bestowing, turning the merely carnal into the spiritual, destroying, in effect, the difference between them. It is this erasure or dissolution of the difference that truly ends duality, turning ordinary mortals into gods and goddesses. Such is the potential and the power of human, sensual, even physical love as demonstrated by Radha and Krishna. The desideratum of *bhakti* is simple: love with *all* your heart and it would be like loving God himself even if the ostensible object of your devotion were a mere man or woman; *bhakti,* ultimately, results in *mukti*. That which binds, that very thing leads to release. The Radha-Krishna story is of loving attachment, rather than detached loving. The latter has been the preferred choice for the spiritually inclined in most cultures, but here we see the rare reversal in which craving itself leads to God-realization. As Siegel points out, 'The religious system aims at release; but human love is bondage and aims at bondage, attachment. In Krsna the paradox of love is realized: bondage is release; the profane dimensions of love are wholly sacred.'[70]

In other words, Radha-Krishna love gives pride of place to a distinctive world of emotional variety, richness, and depth—love's tremulous longings, its multitudinous fears, its endless hopes, its heart-wrenching sorrows, and its mind-blowing ecstasies. Just as sensual and sexual pleasure is an aid to self-realization, so is the whole range of human emotions, which need not be shunned, but directed by love to the highest object, that of obtaining a lasting and transforming union with the beloved. The Supreme Goddess, the Divine Mother, thus infiltrates and re-engineers the male-dominant creed of the Vaishnavas as Radha. Without such an injection of Shakti (power), Vaishnavism could never have reached the heights that it did. But Shaktism gains too: Radha flowers not as Mother but paramour, lover, spouse. That is how Radha adds to the repertoire not only of Vaishnavism but of Tantricism as well. In support, one might argue that the *gopis* are only the older yoginis of Tantricism, pastoralized and tamed. Instead of wild, powerful, and at times destructive energies, they are now docile cowgirls pining for Krishna. The fiercely matriarchal and feral spirits have now been domesticated in the new agriculturalist patriarchy in which women's generative and sexual power is no longer feared or worshipped. What makes Radha so exceptional is that she is God(ess) not as father, mother, child, sibling, or spouse, but as paramour, lover, beloved. The distinction between licit and illicit love is erased in *madhurya;* only love reigns supreme.

Radha is the classic *abhisarika*, the woman who ventures in storm and rain, overcoming both shame and fear, to meet her lover. But here she is exalted to the status of a Goddess for doing so, not stoned, lynched, pronounced whore, or forced to commit suicide. Radha's devotional and sexual prowess is celebrated, even venerated. In her wake there are texts such as *Radhika Santwanam* of Muddupalani, famously quoted by Susie Tharu and K. Lalitha in their Introduction to *Women Writing in India,*[71] where Krishna is taught how to satisfy Radha, which is one of his duties as her lover. Here, the libidinal drive of a woman is not only acknowledged but is shown to demand fulfilment from her male counterpart. Radha's story suggests that the eternal feminine can never be fully suppressed, but rises in one guise or another to claim her rightful equality with the male principle as enshrined in Sankhya, one of India's oldest philosophical traditions. Radha also represents *advaita* or non-dualism simplified. Doctrinally, *advaita*, as propounded by Sankara and others is quite deep and subtle philosophically. But the Radha-Krishna relationship, modelled as it is on romantic human love, is easy for all to comprehend. The divine pair thus embody *advaita* or *advya*—non-duality and non-separation—in a concrete and easy to understand form, Vedanta compressed and personified. Radha-Krishna in Vrindavan is thus the iconic depiction of the initial wholeness which the Upanishads declare as the nature of the ultimate reality: '*purnamada, purnamidam, purnat purnamudachyate...*'

To go back to Gandhi, then, this way of loving does not bind the subject in the chains of causality or trap one in the endless eddies of *samsara*. Instead it is a special kind of *maya*, which in traditional Krishnology goes by the name of Yogamaya. As Edwin F. Bryant explains:

> Yogamaya covers the pure liberated souls in the lila with her power of illusion, such that they are unaware of Krishna's real nature and thus relate to him not as God but rather as their friend, lover, or child, and so on. Were Yogamaya not to extend her influence in this way, the souls would realize Krishna's true nature and be incapable of interacting with him in lila in these intimate ways. To put it differently, how could God truly play spontaneously and unceremoniously with anyone in the role of a son or friend, if everyone knew he was really God? Unlike that of her samsaric counterpart, Yogamaya's power of illusion, then, is a highly desirable and positive one obtained only by the highest yogis.[72]

That is why, of all modes of bhakti or devotion, *madhurya*, the way of regarding the Lord as lover, partner, and spouse is the best. Hence the Vaishnava Goswamis did not hesitate to endorse the contemplation of the erotic sport of Radha-Krishna as the highest object of worship. As Jiva Goswami said,

> So in conclusion it is evident that, though it has generally been presented that Krishna is the supreme form of Godhead, worship of Him in the association of Radha and engaged in amorous pastimes with her is the highest of all.

But Mahatma Gandhi also believed that such worship may not be temperamentally suited to all devotees.

Radha, holding her own ground, might speak up thus: 'Bapu, to love Krishna the way I do, to long to hear the notes of his flute, to wait for days just to catch a glimpse of him, to desire above all to touch him, dance with him, dissolving in his embrace, quickening the very rhythm of one's heart, to be one with him, to experience the joy of union with him, to transcend all separation from him, to think, touch, taste, and hear only him, to speak only him, to praise, worship, exalt only him, and to be teased, touched, abandoned and re-united with him, to be his and to make him one's own, to conquer him, win his favour, subdue his fiercely independent nature—all this is also *brahmacharya*—the way of the vast. To love is also to grow vast, to love not only in the celibate, impersonal way, but to love in a deeply sensual, sexual, and whole-being way, to love personally, even "romantically," is also to lose one's moorings and grow infinite, the circumference of one's being expanding till it embraces the whole cosmos. This, Bapu, is also a way of loving, a way of being, a way to reach God, not only through self-denial, chastity, and renunciation, but also through the fullest participation in the *ananda-yajna*—blissful sacrifice—that is life.'

Love, Longing, and Desire

A *Nayika's* Tale

ALKA PANDE

> Woman is the sacrificial fire,
> the lips of her yoni the fuel,
> the hairs around them the smoke,
> and the vagina itself the flame.
> The act of penetration is the lighting,
> the feelings of pleasure are the sparks.
> In this fire the gods offer up semen-seed,
> and from this offering man is born.
>
> —*Brihadaranyaka Upanishad*

As the *nagarvadhu* ('bride of the city') of Pataliputra, I feel the power of this verse. My father allowed me the freedom to live my life as a woman who chooses not to be bound to the whims and fancies of one man. I am Amrapali, the great dancer, the most seductive and powerful courtesan of the land, the muse of poets and artists, and the inspiration for every young woman who wishes to live her life independently, not subjugating herself to any man. I am Amrapali, who chooses her men with care, finesse and her free will.

Illustration: Anil Relia, Ahmedabad

However, my journey did not start quite like this. I was born to a wealthy and noble father and a beautiful mother who was well versed in the arts. I grew up surrounded by the love and adoration of my parents since I was the only child. My father talked to me about the politics of the state and power of money. My strong and beautiful mother who was as spiritual as she was talented in the fine arts, particularly music, taught me all she knew. I absorbed every bit of information from my two very unusual parents, who were like chalk and cheese in their temperament but very connected in their family values and love for their only child.

Absorbing everything around me, I grew up to be an unusually gorgeous, gifted, and highly intelligent woman. The news of my astounding beauty and talent spread far and wide. I was wooed by kings and princes. Many royal battles were fought over me. I was also trained in the art of lovemaking by the greatest teachers of sexual delight. My only husband, a powerful king, was so delighted with my expertise that he refused to take another wife in spite of the many pressures on him to form dynastic alliances. He was smitten by my beauty, by my ability to arouse the highest sexual desire within him, to take him to the golden heights of orgasmic delight. I was also his charioteer in his battles and royal hunts and provided a keen listening ear to his political strategies, sometimes providing him with a much-needed clue to sort out a tangled web of political intrigue.

The neighboring king and my husband's strongest ally started desiring me and chased me with fervent ardor. One day, I almost fell for his chase, but my sense of dharma, inculcated in me by my father, prevented me from doing so. I felt I had a charmed life until, one day, tragedy befell me.

My handsome, powerful husband died and I was a widow. Swarms of kings and droves of wealthy men started flooding my door once again. I was still young and beautiful, but now I was also a jewel in the crown. I had experience in every walk of life and most importantly I was a giver of the sexual raptures.

While the line of suitors grew outside my palace, the people of the city of Pataliputra petitioned me and also my father that I should not be tied to any one man again. I should share my knowledge of the art of love freely with the men and women of the city. I relented, and I became free. It was I who decided who I would sleep with, share my bed with; I would be bound to no one. I also started a centre where I would train young women in the arts of love and fine arts, and thus I became Amrapali, the *nagarvadhu* or 'bride of the city' of Pataliputra.

For years, I ruled as the queen of desire, as the mistress of seduction, and the rich and powerful men wrestled with each other to catch my eye. Pataliputra adored me. All my suitors, even the ones that I discarded, relished the time they shared with me. So when the sage Vatsyayana started collating his iconic work *Kamasutra*, a compendium of the many aphorisms, the 'sutras' of the seven sages, who each compiled one of the seven books, he came to me to review his theoretical findings. I read all the seven books, and my experiences transformed the book from a compendium of living a deeply enriched and sexually fulfilled life to much more: strategies of romance, love, longing, desire, seduction, and an unabashed valorization of carnal love. The following pages reveal my own interrogation of the *Kamasutra* as I tried to piece together the theoretical discourse of Vatsyayana's *Kamasutra* and my own personal experience.

The *Kamasutra* thus became a book of pleasure, where the individual's lust, sexual prowess and desire are celebrated as never before. It was I who, through my years of lived experience as a wife, lover, courtesan, and *nagarvadhu* helped Vatsyayana string the seven books of thirty-six verses into the *adbhuta*—the wondrous compendium—which ultimately validated both sexual pleasure and a deeply ethical and joyous life suffused with *dharma, artha, kama* and finally, *moksha*.

Central to the *bhakti marga*, a path of complete surrender to God, who epitomized love: love for *atma* and *parmatma*, love for the boy Krishna in the practice of *vatsalya* in *pushtimarg* where Krishna is worshipped as a child, to the divine lovers Radha and Krishna. The ideal manifestation of this is the *Gitagovinda*, a single long poem by the twelfth-century poet Jayadeva, which immortalized divine love. In India, every god has a consort and in the mythic and Puranic traditions, conjugal love is legitimate. In addition to Radha and Krishna, there are Shiva and Parvati, Rama and Sita, Riddhi and Siddhi with Ganesha, Surya with Sandhya and Chaya, and the list continues.

Artists through their *kalpana* (imagination), after reading the *Kamasutra* and the subsequent Kama texts, illustrated a number of pleasure albums which were commissioned by kings and wealthy merchants for their own pleasures. Therefore, it is not surprising that love couples or *dampatya* scenes became a part of the temple embellishments, particularly during the Medieval period which was also the high point of *bhakti*. The sculpting of *mithuna* (couples in loving postures) and *maithuna* couples (in positions of sexual union) goes back to the text of the *Kamasutra* by Vatsyayana, where love, longing, and desire are validated and valorized.

When Vatsyayana shared the first draft of the *Kamasutra*, I saw the broad scope and ambition of the text. I also realized that since it was the first text of its kind, compiled around the third century BC, it would definitely be considered the mother of all erotic writing in India in the years to come. It was the first systematic text on erotic and carnal desires. Ever since Vatsyayana first collated it, it would become the muse for a number of writers and artists, since within its pages was enshrined the essence of marital bliss, consummation of desire, love, longing and even lust. The *Kamasutra* valorizes desire. It is not only about the physical consummation but a total consummation where the mind and body are complete in a shared passion. Desire predates the *Kamasutra*, and is part of the very lifeblood of the *Kamashastras*, which is the generic term for a number of Sanskrit texts which deal with the politics and philosophy of the erotic.

While re-reading the many drafts of Vatsyayana's text I started contemplating the *raison d'etre* of this unusual document, this encyclopedia of human emotional behavior. What is the *Kamasutra*: Is it a book of sexual acrobatics, where men stand on their heads, having sex with multiple women? Is it a book of orgiastic delight, where a man is satisfying three women at the same time? Is it a book of same-sex love? Is it a book of aphrodisiacs where men and women are in a state of inebriated pleasure? Is it a book which helps men to have large extended penises and then turns them into stallions of sexual energy?

What I gathered was that the *Kamasutra* is an album of the wisdom of India's enlightened pre-modern sages which can still stand the test of time. One of the first sages to reflect on the topics covered by the *Kamasutra* was Shvetaketu, son of Uddalaka, during the eighth century BC, who produced a summary of Nandi's utterances. Nandi is not just the sacred bull of Lord Shiva but also his constant companion: during the period between the third and first centuries BC, the vast nature of Shvetaketu's work led many literary scholars/sages to continue the reflections on his work.

I, Amrapali, started my own personal understanding of the text and this is how I deconstructed it. The etymology of the word *kama* can be traced to the divine Hindu god of love known as Kamadeva. The *Arthashastra* is regarded as a text on the principles of politics and governance, and the *Kamasutra* is read as literature to instruct the *nagarika* or townsman in sexual pleasure. Nandi the sacred bull, Shiva's doorkeeper, is attributed with the very first transmission of the treatise. For the benefit of mankind, Nandi recorded the sacred utterances by eavesdropping on the lovemaking of the god Shiva and his wife Parvati.

From there Prajapati, the creator, passed down the *Kamasutra* as a code of conduct in 10,000 chapters. Nandikeshvara, a devotee of Shiva, then took 1,000 chapters on sex from this and revealed them to Shvetaketu Aruni, who condensed the work to 500 chapters in the eighth century BC. This date is based on the idea that Shvetaketu helped to write the *Brihadaranyaka Upanishad* and *Chandogya Upanishad*, which are generally believed by scholars to have been compiled at this time. The ancient sexologist Babhravya attempted to condense Shvetaketu's work into a further reduced text of erotology consisting of 150 chapters. Babhravya made two important innovations. The first was the remarkable sixty-four lovemaking techniques and the second was that he divided his work into seven distinct books. Each of these seven books was then elaborated upon by seven sages, each a specialist in one aspect of the carnal desires. Vatsyayana then compiled the *Kamasutra* from the writings of these sages.

Part of the enigma of the *Kamasutra* is its purpose. I found that Vatsyayana wrote the *Kamasutra* in such a way that while it is a manual for a blissful married life, the seven books also contain codes for experiencing the myriad hues and emotions of a sensual and erotic life. It is for this reason that one of the seven books is devoted to the wives of other men and the ways to seduce them. Did Vatsyayana intend this section as a method of training husbands? Or is it a meditation on the complexities of married life and the way a husband has to be incessantly vigilant? Is the *Kamasutra* simply a sex manual? The Indian philosophy of the *purusharthas*, 'the four main goals of life', is reflected in the *Kamasutra*. *Dharma* holds the highest place, followed by *artha*, which is the vehicle of a comfortable life, *kama* is aesthetic pleasure, and the practice of all three leads to *moksha*.

1. *Dharma*: Virtuous Living

Dharma is the path of a righteous life, where spirituality reigns supreme. It is also adherence to the *Shastras*. Dharma is supposed to be learned from the *shruti* (Holy Writ) and from those familiar with it.

2. *Artha*: Material Prosperity

Artha is the acquisition of arts, land, gold, cattle, wealth, equipages and friends. It is material wealth which is obtained by personal work and merit and not inherited. *Artha* is supposed to be learned from the king's officers and from merchants, who are well-versed in the ways of commerce.

3. *Kama*: Aesthetics and Pleasure

Kama is love, and the emotional feeling of attachment. This can be enjoyment through the five senses of hearing, feeling, seeing, tasting and smelling, assisted by the mind as well as the soul.

4. *Moksha*: Liberation

Moksha may be described as salvation. In Hinduism, liberation from the bondage of worldly action is predicated on detachment and freedom. A judicious balance of the three goals of life—*dharma, artha* and *kama*—leads to the final attainment of *moksha*. An enlightened reading of the *Kamasutra* provides wisdom to help lead a life replete with ethical pleasure. The *Kamasutra* is thus not a manual written by and for a hedonist.

*

My many readings of the *Kamasutra* made me aware of the *nayak* or *nagarika*. The *nagarika* is an archetypical man who is well-versed in the art of love. This is, to a large extent, based on my experience and journey of life. The *nayika,* on the other hand, has numerous manifestations—she could be a coy maiden, a seductress, or demure wife. One of the endearing qualities of the *Kamasutra* is that it is said to come from a time when women were treated as equals and were as entitled as men to sexual pleasure. The *Kamasutra* provides an exhaustive list of accomplishments that a courtesan was expected to have. Aside from music, dance, acting and singing, she was to be versed in architecture, clay modeling, composing poetry, different languages and philosophy. She also had to know flower arranging, making perfumes and cosmetics, conjuring tricks, riddles and tongue twisters, embroidery, cooking, gardening, and teaching parrots and mynahs to talk. Further, she needed to be skilled in chemistry, mineralogy, carpentry, sorcery, writing in code, teaching cocks, partridges and rams to fight, fencing, archery and gymnastics.

The *Kamasutra* is truly more than just a sex manual. In fact, only one of the seven books or parts is about sexual positions. The rest of it is on lessons for a good life, including tips on seduction and maintaining personal grooming, and the importance of physical and emotional health. It is because I had mastery of these qualities that I was given the title of *nagarvadhu*.

- Book One: Sadharana (General Principles) by Charayana
- Book Two: Samprayogika (Love Play) by Suvarnanabha
- Book Three: Kanya Samprayuktaka (Courtship and Marriage) by Ghotakamukha
- Book Four: Bharyadhikarika (The Wife) by Gonardiya
- Book Five: Paradarika (Seducing the Wives of Others) by Gonikaputra
- Book Six: Vaishika (The Courtesan) by Dattaka
- Book Seven: Aupanishadika (Secret Lore) by Kuchumara

What endeared the *Kamasutra* to me was that while it placed a great deal of emphasis on pleasure, it did not preach hedonism. The seven books of the *Kamasutra* are split into thirty-six chapters and sixty-four topics, but I will be concentrating on Books Two, Three, Five, Six, and Seven. Occasional verses, in *shloka* form, are included. They change the meter of the text and are far more expansive than the graphic language of most of the *Kamasutra*. Though not attributed to any particular author or sage, these aphorisms give a personal insight into the text, often in an ironic, even indirect way, and thus give a more prescriptive, and more opinionated, twist.

There are ten chapters to Book Two, Samprayogika (Love Play):

- Compatibility
- Embraces
- Kisses
- Nail marks and Love bites
- Love Positions
- Role Reversal
- Love Blows and Love Cries
- Odd Pleasures
- How to begin and how to end lovemaking
- Lovers' Quarrels

It is concerned principally with sex and descriptions of its variations. Vatsyayana first describes how a man and woman should be matched before sex takes places. He then lists types of position, stages of bliss, and details of kissing, modes of foreplay, types of pleasure, oral sex methods and geographical variations of all of these. When he describes oral sex, Vatsyayana describes what he terms the 'third nature': homosexual relations. The openness with which he describes and does not condemn homosexuality gives a glimpse into the conservatism of later periods. The sixty-four sexual arts are alluded to within this chapter.

Book Three, Kanya Samprayuktaka, (Courtship and Marriage) has five chapters:

- Choosing a Bride
- Winning her Confidence
- Courting Games

- Courting tricks and Strategies
- Love Marriage

After describing the best techniques of sexual fulfillment, Vatsyayana sets out the procedure of meeting somebody with whom the reader can practice them. He begins by describing the right and unsuitable 'types' of women. Once it has been established that intentions are directed correctly, he recounts how the overtures of love should be made, and how each sex could and should conduct themselves. He lists the types of courting situations, how one should be dressed for these, the ways to win the desired good opinion and how women's reactions to these techniques should be understood. Perhaps a little hastily, he describes how the wife's trust should be won following the marriage, and when and how the first sexual encounter should take place. After this, he describes how the engagement should be carried out, giving the reader a glimpse into contemporary rituals.

What I further observed was that Books Three, Four, and Five have overlaps in representation due to the nature of the themes. From courtship to marriage to other men's wives, the women become the central figures. Therefore both men and women are shown in their initial stages of intimacy.

Book Five, Paradarika (Seducing the Wives of Others) has yet another intriguing discussion on polygamy and how it should be played out, with whom, and the possibilities in a harem. It deals with why adultery occurs and the numerous stages of desire that have passed before infidelity occurs. The women play an active role in choosing whether or not to engage in disloyalty. It is not assumed that a man can have any women he chooses. This book has six distinct divisions:

Illustration: Anil Relia, Ahmedabad

- Seducing a Woman
- Illicit Love
- Testing her Feelings
- The Arts of the Go-between
- The Wives of Subordinates
- Breaking into the Harem

What is interesting in the *Kamasutra* is the divergent types of women, and advice to women in channeling their love strategies. Emphasis is laid on seduction, wooing and how the woman reacts to such attention. If she resists a man's advances, Vatsyayana has advice on how these resistances may be overcome. It is important to note that these are not physical resistances, but moral resistance. Following this is a warning to powerful men to not let their power lead to improper conduct with 'available' women, and a list of who may 'have' them. Vatsyayana pre-empts his book on courtesans by describing the sex life of the harem and how an outsider can get inside to enjoy it. As in all matters it is hard to know whether he is recommending this, despite the dangers that would inevitably come from carrying out what has been advised. He lists the geographical differences in harems and what kind of men should be harem guards. Taboos are treated with a great deal of sensitivity and wit.

Book Six, Vaishika (Courtesan) contains six chapters on the selection of lovers, searching for a secured lover, ways of creating finance, reinvigorating a relationship with a former lover, occasional gains and deficits. The six chapters are:

- Choosing a Lover
- Looking for a Steady Lover
- How to Milk a Wealthy Lover
- Making up with a Past Lover

- The End of an Affair
- Financial Transactions Within the Love Game

This chapter appealed to me immensely. In my opinion, a courtesan is a tremendously empowered woman. I felt that Vatsyayana goes into great detail when describing the life of the courtesan, and lays the contemporary practice bare for the reader. He gives detailed accounts of how a courtesan may be recognized, who could be a special client, clients that should be avoided, the differences in why ordinary women and courtesans sleep with men, techniques that courtesans should employ to please a lover, their actions when they are with their lovers, ways of extracting money and gifts from a lover, how the courtesan is to act when a lover is 'cooling off', how they are to get rid of a lover and wealth accrual and business methods. He also informs the reader of the two reasons courtesans sleep with men—pleasure and money—and how this differs for each lover. He then describes what methods the courtesan uses to secure these lovers. Practical advice is given to help the courtesan decide whether it is worth taking back a lover after he has left and ultimately it is accepted that the courtesan makes the final decision about her business. In direct reference to this, there is even a section about how the courtesan should price her services.

Book Six is one of the high points of the *Kamasutra*, particularly for the feisty empowered woman. It is as if the courtesan, the woman, has come of age, she is confident because she is extremely talented, creative and intelligent. It is she who conducts all her financial dealings with her patrons and even discarded lovers.

Book Seven, Aupanishadika (Secret Lore) deals with aphrodisiacs and spells.

This book has two chapters:

- Love Potions and Sex Aids
- Vatsyayana's Blessings

Book Seven is almost magical in its large menu of aphrodisiacs and spells. The final book begins with the revelation that the *Kamasutra's* lessons are over and that the following will help the reader achieve the desired ends. With my help and inputs, Vatsyayana lists recipes and methods for making oneself attractive, making one's daughter attractive to prospective husbands, increasing virility, reviving passion, piercing the penis and enlarging the penis. All of these are relevant to parts of the books that have come before. Recipes, which were often placebos, added zest to the libido and stirred desire to untamed heights.

*

In the above narrative, the tracing of the theoretical discourse of the *Kamasutra* becomes the key to the myriad inclusions of human social behavior and the *raison d'etre* of the writing of the *Kamasutra*. The true understanding of the *Kamasutra* is impossible without drawing upon the history of its narrative. Once the reading of the *Kamasutra* is approached in a systematic manner, it is only then that it is understood to its fullest—not as a sexual-yogic manual but a handbook of living life to its fullest. This marks another stage of the *Kamasutra's* odyssey, which endorses openness to desire and pleasure-seeking activities. It does not need to be 'swallowed whole' and learned in its entirety—those parts of it which can enhance or stimulate the reader's life, in any aspect, can be 'nibbled' at.

See Bibliography on page 204.

Swipe Me Left, I'm Dalit

CHRISTINA DHANARAJ

Many of us are familiar with the statistics from 2014 on OkCupid, which showed that Black women were considered the least romantically desirable group[73] (Asian men were rated lowest by single women). In India, there is no survey yet to explain a similar situation for Dalit women. What love means to us and how our social locations play a role in determining the success of our relationships have, so far, been questions of limited interest.

My dating experiences began when I was in college. I met my first romantic partner around the same time I was beginning to identify as a feminist. This was also when I was coming to terms with my Dalit identity—something I was sure would never threaten the relationship. I believed love conquered everything, just like on celluloid. If a Latina maid in Manhattan could find her happily ever after with a White senatorial candidate in a Hollywood movie, and an upper-caste Shekhar could find everlasting love with a Muslim Shaila Banu in the Mani Ratnam-directed Bollywood movie, surely I could too?

I couldn't have been farther from the truth. After many relationships, I've now come to realise that not only can caste play a role in determining the success of one's romantic pursuit, it can also shape one's competence, desirability, and confidence within a relationship. And love, contrary to what we have been taught, may not be the most sacred of all feelings, insulated from the world and pure in its expression; it is a choice that we make based on who we are and where we come from.

Our attraction for another is a function of our social locations, defined by caste, class, race, and religion. Our decision in choosing a companion is dependent on how reluctant we are to challenge status quos. My then-partner chose to break up with me because his parents couldn't accept the fact that I was Dalit. Another very pointedly told me that his family might be able to accept me if I didn't behave *like a Dalit*.

My own experiences with romantic love, my family's experiences in arranging a marriage for me and my sibling, and my observations on how my fellow Dalit sisters have been treated and perceived in the context of both traditional marriages and modern-day dating, has taught me that loving and being loved, in all its glorified beauty, is a matter of privilege.

Dating in India Today

Most of my women friends whom I grew up with in school and college got into arranged marriages, and very few dated to find their partners. Those that are unmarried today are still looking at arranged marriage as a potential route. My family has also been asked to try that. But given that we had very limited access to social networks, we put up profiles on both elite and not-so-elite web portals, specifying everything but our caste. Proposals came from different types of families and men, both from India and overseas, with one question in common: What is your caste?

In 2014, the first direct estimate of inter-caste marriage in India said that only five per cent[74] of Indians married a person from a different caste. If India is embracing modernity[75] and a new breed of Indo-Anglians[76] are emerging, is it possible that the remaining ninety-five per cent is not using just the arranged marriage method to find intra-caste partners? Is it possible that Indians are looking for intra-caste prospects via modern dating methods as well?

Over the past few years, there have been a slew of stories on how apps like Tinder are revolutionizing the matrimonial space in India, where matches are supposedly made not on the basis of caste.[77] While it is true that these apps do not ask for one's caste (like matrimonial websites do), these don't necessarily ensure that a legal or a social inter-caste union will take place. Apps like Tinder are only casting a wider net to have *access* to people from different castes, thereby creating an illusion of breaking barriers. Offline, people still legitimize their unions based on caste markers, such as surnames, localities, dialects, parents' jobs, religion, economic status, political and pop culture idols, food choices, ideology, and skin colour.

Feminist Discourse on Modern Dating

There is also a steady stream of discourse dedicated to how Indian women are gaining sexual agency, in that they are no longer hesitant when it comes to casual sex,[78] being with married men,[79] or having an open relationship.[80] Hook-ups and casual dating, via an app or otherwise, are perceived to be creating a sex-positive culture for Indian women who may otherwise be inhibited from experiencing unbridled sexual pleasure inside or outside of a relationship. Unsurprisingly, this mainstream feminist discourse is predominantly led by women from upper-caste/bourgeoise locations. Not all Dalit women (cisgender, heterosexual, urban, and educated), who consider dating as a possible route to finding romantic partners, necessarily share the same experience.

At the heart of a good, intimate relationship is the understanding that those involved in sustaining that bond are of value. But how is this value determined and who in the relationship determines it? The highest value, as defined by Hinduism, has traditionally been ascribed to the Brahmin woman, followed by the Kshatriya, the Vaishya, and the Shudra. The modern-day ideal is also a savarna or a savarna-passing woman, who is typically light-skinned and able-bodied, belonging to a family that has monetary and social capital, and embodying qualities considered to be feminine. The farther one is from this ideal, the more undervalued she is perceived to be. Within relationships, this perception, albeit external, translates into an unhealthy power imbalance, leading to a potential compromising of one's rights, desires, and authenticity.

Dalit women who carry the double burden of gender and caste, and are one of the most socially undervalued in India, are therefore under constant pressure to project an acceptable version that mimics the savarna ideal. In a romantic pursuit or a partnership, we are expected to operate along a behavioral band that is far narrower than what is required of a non-Dalit woman. Needless to say, the existence of this ever-present mandate to be something one is not, so as to constantly prove one's value or romantic potential, even in the most personal of spaces that is ideally supposed to feel like home, is unfair at best and cruel at worst. And the price that is asked of us, in return for a semblance of normalcy, is our safety, dignity, and mental health.

Seeking Love When Dalit and Woman

While I do not know of every Dalit woman's experience, I can say (based on mine and that of my friends/ acquaintances) that dating in India overall is nowhere close to the rosy picture characterized by the absence of caste or the prominence of female sexual agency. Dalit women are repeatedly stereotyped as:

- *Victims*: We are primarily viewed as victims and survivors of various kinds of violence.[81] Reification of the Dalit identity has led to the boxing of our existence, whose dimensions are solely defined by the savarna gaze.[82] Our self-assertions of identity are commodified to create a warped limiting of our lives, in effect creating an image that is helpless and voiceless in the minds of our potential suitors. We are not seen as being capable of desire, love, or happiness; we don't seem to exist as *individuals* outside of violence.

  Not only does this make us seem unattractive, especially in the context of dating where confidence is generally regarded as an attractive trait, but it also has further implications in an actual romantic or sexual relationship. Because it is assumed that we do not have the power to protect ourselves, our bodies and our labour are grossly undervalued. Intimate violence may follow, whose magnitude is further aggravated by a real (or perceived) lack of monetary and social support in the case of under-privileged Dalit women.

While traditional discourses, most often authored by savarna voices, have concluded that we face intimate violence only at the hands of Dalit men (which in turn has led to the unfair criminalizing of Dalit men and boys), our lived realities today speak of another truth. Non-Dalit male partners are far more likely to inflict violence on us both physically and sexually, for the reason that they face far less legal and social consequences when reported.

- *Unfeminine*: The Dalit woman is perceived mostly in comparison to her non-Dalit counterpart: the lighter-skinned savarna woman who is pure, quiet and delicate, versus the dark-skinned Dalit woman who is polluting, loud and tough. Pop culture through the ages has helped propagate this dichotomy. By casting only light-skinned savarna women as love interests of the male protagonist, it has implied that the one deserving of love and a happily ever-after will need to have a certain set of physical attributes and come from a certain social location. Even in the case of Dalit male protagonists, the one who catches his eye or steals his heart is most often not a Dalit woman (Sairat, Thalapathy, Kadhal), who *when* represented, is often depicted as loud-mouthed, angry, and verbally abusive.

  In the real world, this translates into an angry Dalit woman stereotype, which lacks femininity and therefore cannot evoke the feeling of romantic love in a heteronormative sexual setting. Particularly in the case of a politicized Dalit woman who is active on social media and the digital space, this stereotype is repeatedly used against her in an effort to invalidate her political critiques. The mere voicing of her opinions and the vocalizing of her lived experiences invites a barrage of accusations from both Dalits and non-Dalits. If such a woman does succeed in finding a heterosexual romantic partner, she is expected to maintain certain behaviours so as to sustain the relationship. These include subscribing to the ideals of a traditional wife/girlfriend, finding ways to integrate herself into the partner's social circle, and leaving her 'identity politics' outside the door.

Thus, in most cis-hetero relationships, the price paid by a Dalit woman (stereotyped as angry and unfeminine) towards its success is far higher than that required of a non-Dalit woman. The latter can retain her political self and still be perceived as feminine, while the former will have to keep proving her femininity by choosing to not voice her political opinions, which are typically deemed as irrational. Voicing of these opinions, either publicly or privately, means the potential end to a relationship.

- *Promiscuous*: The dichotomy of the Dalit vs. Non-Dalit woman also shapes how the former is perceived and treated sexually. As Rowena points out,[83] the upper-caste woman's body is regarded as sacred, protected by the men in her family, based on notions of chastity, virginity and docile femininity. But the Dalit woman's body has traditionally been regarded as a site of sexual pleasure and entertainment without the need for legitimacy. She says, 'upper caste women are constantly imagined and represented as chaste and sexually controlled, in opposition to lower caste women who are repeatedly portrayed as sexually loose, hyper and "immoral," a process that starts right from the differences in the representations of Sita and Shoorpanakha in the Ramayana.'

Today's urban Dalit woman navigating the modern dating/matrimonial space is not spared this stereotyping. What the sexually liberated non-Dalit woman does and articulates is accepted as a credible political response,[84] while what the Dalit woman does is perceived as shameful.[85] Casual sex, being with married men, and having open relationships, which are touted as sexually liberating and indicative of a sex-positive culture does not hold the same meaning for Dalit women. Particularly in the case of men having savarna women as partners, their interest in Dalit women outside of the legitimate relationship is only an urban/modern version of upper-caste men sexually exploiting disadvantaged Dalit women that work in their fields/houses. In most cases, the savarna partner is not threatened by this arrangement; she continues to be the legitimate entity in the equation while the Dalit woman is relegated to the task of satisfying the man's unconventional sexual desires.

Where Do We Go from Here?

The stereotyping that Dalit women face when navigating the modern dating space is likely to be far more sinister than what I have described above. And the more *aware* she becomes of the dynamics, the tougher it becomes for her to trust—a key ingredient needed in finding and sustaining a loving relationship.

She is constantly under pressure to project an acceptable version that should be sexy but not loose, docile but not weak, confident but not too strong, lest she be stereotyped, only to be further exploited or victimized. Lack of social capital or support, in the form of friends or family, also makes it difficult when dealing with break-ups or legitimizing social unions.

Although this subject requires more in-depth articulation in terms of what we can do as individuals, allies, families, and communities, I believe it is important to start with the following:

1. Rethink the discourse around polyamory, open relationships and casual sex in the context of modern heterosexual relationships. Although these are, by definition, sex positive and may work as liberal alternatives for mainstream feminists who come from privileged social locations, it could potentially be exploitative for Dalit women.
2. As progressive communities, it is important to love and cherish Dalit women for who they are and what they are becoming. Constantly prioritizing the fragility of non-Dalit women or choosing to perceive them as the ones worthy of romantic love or legitimacy are typical ways in which Dalit women are undervalued in private spaces. This must stop.
3. Have a serious discourse on the politics of desirability within the Indian context. Who we choose to have sex with, be 'friends with benefits' with, and then go

on to have committed, exclusive relationships with, are political. This cannot be downplayed as personal preference.[86] Social location by virtue of caste, race, class, religion, ethnicity, and other markers plays a huge role in determining our romantic and sexual choices.

4. Actively challenge the dominance of the savarna and the cis-hetero male gaze, which continues to propagate the Madonna/Whore dichotomy in its various cultural manifestations, desires only certain types of bodies, and pigeonholes Dalit women as irrationally angry women or other stereotypes as described above.
5. We are a long way off from creating a world that values Dalit women in both the public and the private space. Modernity has not ensured an egalitarian world for everyone. Unless we are willing to seriously question our privileges across every space, our role in holding up negative stereotypes of Dalit women, and our personal choices in love and sex, what we do in the name of anti-caste politics will only be performative.

Apps do not kill caste; we do.

Love Jihad

NILANJAN MUKHOPADHYAY

Much before it became an institution of hate for Hindu extremist groups, New Delhi's Jawaharlal Nehru University in the 1970s and '80s provided space for students like me to participate in so-called 'wrongful' activities. These included assisting friends from different communities and faiths to marry each other and thereby be 'morally justified' to use condoms, which are allegedly cast away by the metric tonne after use on the campus.[87] Interfaith marriages were common at that time on campus. One such match in my close circle did not meet with opposition in either family; they only wanted the respective faiths to be 'respected'. The marriage, eventually solemnized a few years after we left university, was arranged in three stages: a Hindu marriage after the groom was temporarily 'converted' to Hinduism, followed by a Nikah ceremony when the bride was likewise 'converted' to Islam, and eventually a civil marriage where the duo signed the marriage register under their own names which still remain unchanged for both! In the middle of 2015, in a sudden quest for humorous banter, I called up the male of the duo. After exchanging polite pleasantries,

I charged him with the following: 'Do you know you are among the original love jihadis?'

He grunted in appreciation at my black humour. But beyond this we did not find it funny anymore, as the consequences of what might happen if he was actually dubbed so dawned on us. Neither of us mentioned it, but we knew the threat he and his family—including their proud son with dual religious identity—would face if the local Mohalla Pramukh or colony-in-charge of the Hindu Suraksha Samiti, Hindu Protection Committee or any other militant Hindu organisation put a marker on their doorway during a campaign against mixed marriages. In just three and a half decades, India seems to have undergone fundamental changes in how, from a time when progressive personal choices, though applauded only by some but surely not chastised by all, were the norm, to a situation where even those who support such decisions are sceptical for fear that their loved ones will come to harm. This worry has become gnawing in the wake of a campaign where generating fear of the other has become a major strategy of Hindu sectarian groups. In response, this tactic has been adopted by minority fundamentalist groups too, though to a much lesser extent.

Love and Jihad *per se* are incompatible words. Yet both Islamists and Hindu sectarian groups use the two words, one after the other and in the same sequence, by treating the two as different parts of speech. Islamists use 'love' as verb and Jihad or jehad as noun, while Hindu chauvinists club the two together and use the phrase either as verb or as noun with the word 'love' acting as the prefix of the other. In one of his media interactions in September 2001 just days after the 9/11 attacks in the United States, Osama Bin Laden told *Ummat*, a Karachi-based Urdu newspaper that his organisation, 'while not involved with the attacks', was not distressed with the freeze on Al Qaeda's accounts because 'with the grace of God, Al Qaeda has more than three alternative financial systems, which are all separate and totally independent of each other. This system is operating under the patronage of those who love Jihad...'[88]

In contrast to this particular usage, Hindu sectarian groups use the two words in a starkly different manner. From 2014 onwards, English newspapers and websites in India have carried an assortment of headlines ranging from "Rape, 'love jihad' top BJP's Muzaffarnagar campaign," "Love Jihad in Vadodara comes with a prize tag of Rs 7L for Sikh girl, Rs 5L for a Brahmin," "Love jihad: WhatsApp message goes viral" to "We Now Have Concrete Proof for Love Jihad," "Man Murdered, Retribution for Love Jihad," "Love Jihad couple move in together" or the headline tagging a video in September 2018: Love Jihad "Meerut Police Assaulting Girl in Van." Love Jihad has now become an essential component in the Hindu rightwing pillorying of Muslims, as evidenced in this November 2018 report: "Tripura: Migrant workers from Assam, Bangladesh involved in love jihad, cow slaughter, claims VHP." What precisely is this form of Jihad that is being used to whip up majoritarian sentiment and what is the historical basis of this?

*

Sexual entrapment and violence against women of the 'other' has historically been a tactic in episodes of mass violence and protracted inter-community conflict. Scholars have examined instances when bodies of women were used as fields for patriarchal lords to wage battles. In South Asia, women were the worst affected during the Partition riots in 1947 with each community attacking women of the others': Muslim women were abducted, kidnapped, molested and raped by Hindu and Sikh men while Muslim men acted similarly against Sikh and Hindu women.[89] In certain cases, women were abducted and after they failed in uniting with their families, converted to the religion of the abductor and stayed with them, either in bondage or in marital relationships. Another large-scale episode of sexual violence against women occurred during the brutal repression of East Pakistan by the army dominated by men from West Pakistan.

After independence, communalism continued to be a recurring phenomenon in Indian politics and episodes of sectarian violence erupted in different parts of India with regularity. In each of these episodes, brutal sexual violence against women of the other community was perpetrated, with the sole exception of the pogrom directed against Sikhs in Delhi and other parts of India in 1984. Perpetrated in the wake of Indira Gandhi's assassination, the primary objective in this bout of communal carnage was to defang or emasculate adult Sikh males.[90] In other instances of sexual violence, women were targeted because they were considered the weakest link of the adversary. Because patriarchy viewed women as property requiring protection by men, sexual subjugation of women was treated as assault on their respective community leaders. Humiliating women thereby became a form of proxy assault on the entire community.

Initially, the desire to sexually possess women was essentially a violent action and not part of the political campaign against another community. The first time that possession of the 'other's' woman became a political objective in independent India was in the late 1980s during the Ram Janambhoomi movement, when supporters of the Vishwa Hindu Parishad's agitation routinely painted graffiti declaring, 'I am the son-in-law of Babur (the Mughal Emperor)' implying that supporters of the agitation had conjugal rights over the daughter(s) of the Mughal emperor, in this instance symbolizing Muslims in contemporary society. The slogan was reflective of the main spirit of the agitation to demolish the Babri Masjid; the mosque had to be removed because it was a symbol of subjugation and humiliation of Hindus over several centuries, and revenge could be taken by conquering the 'prized possession', i.e. the daughter of the patriarch. In the course of the agitation, several rabid youth groups, while making their way to Ayodhya, frequently raised slogans demeaning female Muslim film actors, presenting them as objects of sexual fantasy. This strategy assisted in increasing support for the campaign, especially among revenge-seeking Hindu supporters.

In fact, there is no gainsaying that sexual 'acquisition' of Muslim women during the Ayodhya agitation was reflective of the inherent sexual undertones of the campaign. After the 1989 Lok Sabha election, when the BJP's strength dramatically increased from 2 seats to 85, the party enjoyed the media spotlight on one of its first-time MPs—a 30-year woman *sanyasin*, Uma Bharati. Journalists gave her the moniker of 'Sexy Sanyasin' and neither party leaders nor she initially objected to it. Saffron-clad Bharati was drawn into the VHP in her youth after her prowess at memorizing religious texts was recognized by its leaders, and she was at the forefront of the Ram temple agitation. During one such protest in October 1990, when the state government imposed prohibitory orders, Bharati reached the temple town in disguise after shearing her hair. A party MP, quoted in my book *The Demolition: India at the Crossroads*,[91] contended that she symbolically compromised her sexual chastity by going bald, an act of penance and self-denial traditionally undertaken by widowed Hindu women. Bharati was in subsequent months joined by other women religious leaders to galvanize support for the agitation. I quoted Sadhvi Rithambara beseeching Hindu men to 'stir out of their impotency and give it back to them.'[92] I further argued that her body language would:

> [O]ften be movements that had strong parallels to the sexual gyrations seen in popular Indian cinema...The two women got religious sanctity from the saffron robes, and their exhortations could not be faulted. They symbolised the 'devi' cult that was trying to restore the lost virility of the Hindu youth.[93]

During the demolition of the Babri Masjid, Bharati was on the stage from where leaders of the BJP and VHP had a ringside view of the demolition. She repeatedly exhorted the demolishers with the slogan, '*ek dhakka aur maaro, Babri Masjid tor do*' ('Give it another push, bring down the Babri Masjid') in a very suggestive manner, full of violent sexual prompts or undertones. The use of sexuality served its purpose and, after the demolition, a campaign was mounted that the Muslims were now 'doing to Hindu women' what was probably the original plan of the Hindutva brigade. This was necessary because the demolition of the Babri Masjid on 6 December 1992 forced Muslims in India to realize what it meant to be a member of a religious minority in the country, and also emboldened Hindus who perceived a tectonic shift in the equation between Hindus and Muslims.

Yet, despite winning that round by altering perceptions of religious minorities for a significant number of Indians and securing greater acceptance for their version of secularism, Hindu sectarian forces were hamstrung by being unable to go beyond the electoral plateau. In 1996, the BJP formed a union government after emerging as the largest party in the Lok Sabha, the Lower House of the Indian Parliament. Yet the government collapsed in less than a fortnight because Indian politics was not yet ready to accept a Hindu sectarian party as the governing outfit. To further strengthen its position and secure support of more sections for the Hindutva idea, the BJP and its affiliates in the Sangh Parivar—the phalanx of organizations owing allegiance to the RSS—raised two bogeys: firstly, the fear of Hindus being outnumbered or demographically swamped by Muslims because the birth rate in absolute terms in the Muslim community was higher than among Hindus. Secondly, a campaign was built that Muslims—and increasingly, Christians were clubbed with the more dominant religious minority—were out to seduce innocent Hindu girls, who were being lured in a planned manner by handsome, lecherous young Muslim men who even raped or sexually coerced Hindu girls by feigning love. The campaign by Hindu sectarian groups began gaining ground from the late 1990s and early years of the twenty-first century. Because in the patriarchal Hindu viewpoint, women—though hallowed as mothers, sisters, daughters and of course, goddesses—were little more than sexual playfields and wombs to further the race, they were not considered as having the capacity—or the right—to enter into consensual relationships with Muslim men.

Men were enlisted in the campaign to prevent erosion of 'Hindu culture' and in post-liberalization India, Hindutva forces were among the main campaigners against celebrations and dating during market-sponsored 'lovefests' on Valentine's Day. Hindu men were lectured on how important it was for them to also act as protectors of Hindu female sexuality and not just in their families. Women too, especially the college-going section, were encouraged to join Durga Vahini, the women's wing of the Vishwa Hindu Parishad which was formed in 1991 as part of the Sangh Parivar's strategy to maximize support for the Ayodhya agitation. However, after the demolition of the Babri Masjid, this organization too moved into social issues, and preventing sexual or social unions between Hindu girls and Muslim boys became one of its primary objectives.

Dibyesh Anand, in his book *Hindu Nationalism in India and the Politics of Fear*, writes that during his field research in several cities and towns in north and western India, he met narrators of 'localized, "factual" stories concerning a disconcerting common theme—the kidnapping of Hindu girls.' As he notes, 'everywhere I was told by narrators that they personally knew of cases where kidnapping of a Hindu girl has been foiled or a kidnapped girl has been rescued by brave Hindutva activists. All the stories were uncannily similar; they were variations on the same theme. This clearly reflects the sharing of vocabulary of mythmaking.'[94]

Among the stories that Anand referred to were several which had similarities to what I heard and read about over the course of almost two decades. In this period, starting with the late 1990s, there were times when the campaign reached high decibel levels while on other occasions, it remained a soft rumble in the social discourse of Hindutva votaries. The stories often failed to disguise the fact that the woman in the tale was actually in love with her Muslim boyfriend or husband. But the way in which the narrative was twisted demonstrated that for many Hindutva activists, a Hindu girl had no right to choose her own partner; and if she was ever condescendingly permitted the privilege, the choice must be a Hindu man and that too from within her own caste.

This anger against Hindu girls who, by choice, entered into a relationship, platonic or otherwise, was exhibited most starkly in September 2018, in the incident referred to previously. In the western Uttar Pradesh city of Meerut—theatre of much communal violence for decades, and where the campaign against Love Jihad has been particularly virulent since 2013—the police intervened after Hindu activists of the VHP were harassing a Hindu nursing student and her Muslim friend at his rented accommodation. A video then surfaced in which the police, instead of escorting the young girl to safety, admonished and assaulted her, with the male constable commenting, while his female colleague thrashed the student: '*Mullah zyada pasand aa raha hai? Woh hi dikh rahe hain Hindu ke hote hue? Mullah ka le rahi ho?*' (Very fond of a Mullah? Despite Hindus being all around, you could find only them? Sleeping with a Mullah?)[95]

This seems to indicate that sexual jealousy towards the stereotypical Muslim man was at the root of the Love Jihad campaign. Envy of the imagined sexual prowess of Muslim men—recall, for instance, the cinematic depiction of Alauddin Khilji in the popular Hindi film of 2018, *Padmaavat*—is thus a core trigger of extremist Hindu prejudice against them, buttressed by claims that Muslim men sleep with more women because having four wives is permissible; their population growth is higher as they do little else but procreate; and so on.

Towards the last years of the nineteenth century, the campaign of *Shuddhi* (purification) and for Hindu *sangathan* (organisation for defence of Hindus) gained currency among many Hindus in north India. The first component of this two-headed campaign was a movement to 'reclaim' those who had converted to Islam or Christianity several generations ago, and was among the principal activities of the Arya Samaj movement. Significantly, women began to be used as pawns in the game to widen the communal schism, and from the 1920s, a campaign was built around alleged 'abductions and conversion of Hindu women by Muslim goondas, ranging from allegations of rape, abduction and elopement, to luring, conversion, love and forced marriages.'[96]

Pamphlets and handbills were uniform in their treatment of Hindu women as innocent and incapable of protecting themselves. The responsibility of protecting these women from Muslims fell on Hindu men, and they were told that failure would mean bringing down their religion. Some of these booklets that Gupta mentioned were titled provocatively: *Hindu Aurton Ki Loot* and *Hindu Striyon ke loot ka karan*. These publicity materials drew heavily from a substantial body of texts available increasingly from the nineteenth century which portrayed medieval Muslim-ruled kingdoms as those which encouraged abduction and conversion of Hindu women. In the 1920s, and also during the post-1990s phase of revival of this vituperative campaign, vigilantism was encouraged by the campaign managers. Several instances began surfacing in the 1990s and have continued since, when self-appointed custodians of Hinduism and Hindu religious morality have threatened Hindu girls to stop them seeing their Muslim boyfriends or even if they are not in any such relationship, disallowed them from moving freely in cities, towns and villages.[97] Quite often the vigilantes were completely off the mark in their accusations. For instance, in June 2009, a girl went missing in Bantwal Taluka in Karnataka. A campaign was launched and a case was made out that one Pakistan-backed Jihadi 'lover' had converted her to Islam. The campaign ran for several months, at the end of which the police arrested a Hindu youth who confessed that he had poisoned the girl. In 2013, he was convicted after being found guilty of being a serial killer. The police had alleged that he killed 21 young girls within five years. His modus operandi was to befriend a girl, marry her and then kill her a day after the marriage by poisoning.[98]

Hindu sectarian politics got its most decisive push after the 2002 Gujarat riots sparked off following the Godhra carnage. After being run without any organisation, and often being confined to just one locality, such vigilantism acquired a more structured form when several organisations mushroomed. These included the Akhil Bharatiya Hindu Suraksha Samiti, Hindu Janjagruti Samiti, Hindu Aikyavedi and Sree Rama Sene—which also attracted notoriety in Mangalore for bashing up young Hindu women for going to pubs in 2009, an incident that generated a wave of protests against such sectarian violence. Though they did not act in mutual cooperation, the issues they raised were mostly similar. The RSS or the BJP was not formally a part of this agitation, but personal association of several leaders with these new outfits was not uncommon. Moreover, senior leaders also resorted to stony silence whenever a controversial statement was made or an offensive act committed. While these focused on a plethora of issues 'plaguing Hindu society,' the greatest importance was laid on preserving the four pillars of Hindu society: cows, temples, ancient culture and girls. But while there were organisations to protect temples and culture, Hindu girls and cows required special attention. Some groups focused on ensuring Hindus girls did not marry (fall in love or elope) outside the religion while others stepped out to protect cows and conducted this campaign which, in time, had horrific consequences like the incident of a Muslim man being lynched in Dadri, Uttar Pradesh, in 2015.

The framework of the argument that Muslims had historically waged Love Jihad against Hindus was built on the primary Hindu sectarian template that Hindus had been wronged since the beginning of 'Muslim rule'. 'Islamic invaders have forcibly converted Hindu women and made them wear burqa' is the opening statement on a Hindu website.[99] This is followed in quick succession by assertions such as:

- In 712 AD, Muhammad bin Qasim captured over 100,000 Hindu girls and auctioned them in the markets of Kabul and Kandahar.
- Mahmud of Ghazni plundered Mathura and sent 70,000 Hindu women to Islamic countries along with the loot. He acted similarly after defeating Hindu kings elsewhere.
- Allauddin Khilji committed atrocities on the 8-year old daughter of a defeated Hindu king.
- Humayun abducted a bride from a Hindu marriage procession.

- Akbar abducted Jodhabai with the sly intention of neutralising Rajputs (as evidence, scripts of commercial Hindi films like *Mughal-e-Azam*, *Anarkali* and *Jodha-Akbar* are cited).
- In modern times, male Muslim film actors marry female Hindu actors—for instance Saif Ali Khan, Shahrukh Khan and Amir Khan.
- Hindu heroines and directors who have 'been victims of Love Jihad' include Sharmila Tagore, Kareena Kapoor, Amrita Singh and Kiran Rao.
- Directors also film love scenes between Muslim heroes and Hindu heroines to create illicit emotions of love.

The Hindu Janajagruti Samiti also published a booklet on Love Jihad, most of its arguments being fairly pedestrian. For instance, inter-faith marriages or relationships cannot be because of love because why does not the 'true lover in such cases convert into a Hindu for the sake of loving the girl?' Or, for instance, 'love-jihad is religious terrorism because such actions are committed by fanatic groups who are also involved in alluring [sic] Hindu girls. Even fanatic girls assist in entrapping Hindu girls. Terrorists are financed by someone; the same way, in love-jihad too, someone is the financer.' HJS and other similar groups—both formal and informal—make these claims without evidence. It has been argued that the objective of Love Jihad is to 'love a Hindu girl within the time frame of two weeks and brainwash them to get converted and marry within six months. If the target won't get trapped within the first two weeks, they are targeted to leave them and move to another girl. College students and working girls should be the primary target. Once their mission is completed, the organisation will give them one lakh rupees and financial assistance for the youth to start a business. Free mobile phones, bikes and fashionable dresses are provided to them as tools for the mission. Money for this Love Jihad comes from the Middle East.'

The campaign against this so-called Love Jihad being waged against Hindus has become more virulent with the passing years and reached a peak as the 2014 parliamentary elections approached. Riots broke out in Muzaffarnagar, Uttar Pradesh in August-September 2013 on a typical issue of sexual harassment of a girl (also called eve-teasing in India, which makes the crime appear less serious or offensive).[100] But this escalated into a major Hindu-Muslim conflict that lasted several months. It became the cause of major communal polarisation in the state and resulted in the BJP sweeping the state, winning an unprecedented ninety per cent plus of the total eighty parliamentary seats in the state.

Love Jihad was integral to the BJP campaign in 2014, and its leading lawmaker and head of a Hindu '*math*' in Gorakhpur, Uttar Pradesh—Yogi Adityanath—claimed that Muslims had launched the plan against Hindu girls and that it was an international conspiracy targeting India. He was placed in charge of important bye-elections in the state after the parliamentary victory, which seems to indicate that Prime Minister Narendra Modi endorsed the tactics which he was known to have used in the past. Muslims 'can't do what they want by force in India, so they are using the love jihad method here,' he spewed during a television debate, this rhetoric becoming central to the election discourse.[101] Vigilante groups mushroomed and they prohibited Hindu girls from using mobile phones. Another BJP lawmaker-cum-religious leader, Sakshi Maharaj, claimed to be in possession of information that each Muslim boy who was successful in seducing one girl would be rewarded with Rs 11 lakh for a Sikh girl, Rs 10 lakh for a Hindu girl and Rs 7 lakh for a Jain girl.[102] The supporters of the BJP also spread canards about a Hindu girl who had been abducted and gang-raped. She later informed the police that she had not been abducted but was in love with the man and eloped with him.[103] Such cases were reported from other parts of India too, and over a considerable spread of time. For instance, in May 2015, a girl in South 24 Parganas district in West Bengal told a court that she ran away from home because her parents physically abused her. The case had been communalised by the BJP, which campaigned that the area's Muslim community had abducted her. But as the girl revealed, it was an instance of elopement rather than abduction: she had run away from home with a Muslim classmate from school.[104]

After evidence began gathering that the theory of Islamists waging Love Jihad against Hindu society had no real basis, the BJP dropped plans to discuss the issue at a party meeting in September 2014. Yet, the official organs of the party's ideological mentor, the Rashtriya Swayamsevak Sangh—*Organiser* and *Panchjanya*—put the controversial issue on the covers of the two weeklies. The cover feature detailed the story of a woman shooter who accused her husband of forcing her to convert to Islam. The caption next to her photo provocatively posed—'Love Jihad: Reality or Rhetoric?' The magazine ran an editorial too, with an accompanying visual depicting a veiled female face; the opening on the eyes and forehead had iron rods to denote that she was in jail. The forehead depicted a *bindi* with drops of blood trickling down.[105]

The Hindi magazine's cover was more inflammatory, with a picture of a man wearing a kaffiyah—the traditional Arab headdress. He sported a beard in the shape of a heart and sunglasses with a reflection of red hearts on them. '*Pyar andha ya dhandha*' (Is love blind or a business), asked the cover.[106]

When Love Jihad became a major contested issue during the bye-polls in Uttar Pradesh, the Allahabad High Court asked the government to investigate and report. Ten days later, the state informed the court that it did not find any evidence that Love Jihad either existed or was being waged by any group. The state police chief also told Reuters that, 'in most cases we found that a Hindu girl and Muslim boy were in love and had married against their parents' will. These are cases of love marriages and not Love Jihad.'[107]

Despite the storm it generated, and the accompanying escalation of a communal campaign by BJP lawmakers, there was no reining in the Hindu sectarian forces. In January 2015, *Himalaya Dhwani* (the Sound of Himalayas), a magazine published by Durga Vahini, morphed a picture of Kareena Kapoor to cover half her face with a burkha, with the headline: Love Jihad—Conversion of Nationality Through Religious Conversion (*Dharmantaran se Rashtrantaran*).[108]

The magazine justified the actor's photo-shopped image, arguing that Kapoor was 'a celebrity. The youth try to emulate celebrities. They think if she can do so, why not us?' The editorial further detailed: 'There has been much debate

■ Magazine on 'love jihad' with Kareena's morphed face.

on love jihad and conversions. The nation was divided and Pakistan was created because of conversions. If a girl gets caught in love jihad and becomes Muslim by mistake and now wants to return to her original faith, isn't it her right? It's strange that some parties claiming to be secular call this conversion.' The last part of the argument was a reference to the *Ghar Wapasi* or 'Homecoming' programme that was contentiously started by the VHP.

Curiously, allegations of Love Jihad, which continued to exert a decisive impact on politics in north India, were also heard in the Muslim-dominated districts of north Kerala which were flush with Gulf money since the late 1980s and early 1990s. In June 2012, the state chief minister, Oommen Chandy, informed the state legislature that 2667 young women had converted to Islam in the state since 2006. The disclosure followed the High Court directive after parents of a Hindu girl filed a habeas corpus plea when their 20-year-old daughter eloped from a hospital in Kochi with a Muslim boy. The figures tabled by Chandy revealed that there were disproportionately higher number of conversions to Islam from Hinduism and Christianity when compared to Muslims who changed their faith. The chief minister asserted that his government found no evidence of forced conversions in the state, and the fears about love jihad were baseless. To a query posed by a Communist Party of India (Marxist) legislator, he declared: 'We will not allow forcible conversions. Nor will we allow anyone to spread hate campaign against Muslims in the name of love jihad.'[109]

Significantly, the National Investigation Agency probed interfaith marriages in Kerala but did not discover any credible evidence of coercion that could result in prosecution in these cases. The investigating agency had been directed by the Indian Supreme Court to investigate the background of eleven cases of interfaith marriage, as part of allegations of an Islamic conspiracy. Even in a case in which the parents of the Hindu girl filed a petition in court—the state High Court annulled the marriage—the apex court in 2018 restored the marriage.[110]

However, allegations of Love Jihad continue to be traded between various religious communities in Kerala. In June 2015, Mathew Anikuzhikkattil, a Catholic Bishop in Idukki, Kerala, alleged that Christian girls were being 'abducted by Love Jihad'—but this time by the Hindu outfit Sree Narayana Dharma Paripalana (SNDP) Yogam. 'Inter-caste marriages would destroy Christian essence and style. Our girls are being abducted by love jihad,' he claimed, adding that girls who opted for inter-caste marriages were abandoning the Christian faith.[111]

Often overlooked in these debates are the sociological reasons behind the skewed conversion rate from one community to another, besides personal choices. For instance, relationships with rich Gulf-returned Muslim men in the Malabar region can turn out to be an escape from poverty or middle-class drudgery for Hindu girls. Similarly, rigid religious diktats can be the reason for others opting for inter-faith relationships. As economic liberalisation has broken several social barriers, so too has access to information. New forms of entertainment and the growth of the infotainment industry has made the youth of today willing to experiment more in personal habits, lifestyle choices, and personal relationships.

For communal groups, such intermingling is a reason for worry because it makes raising the 'fear of the other' a much more difficult and time-consuming task. Yet social prejudices are so ingrained in Indian society that the slightest endorsement from the state or ruling party to keep building barriers between communities will hamper the emergence of a modern approach to romance and love, and thereby a modern India. The Kerala Bishop was vehement in his assertion that the faithful should oppose inter-faith and inter-caste relationships. A similar view is held by the Hindu and Muslim orthodoxy, and those who practice communal politics of any hue.

Ironically, love can be expressed in generous doses without fear and Jihad can be fought back with determination if there are more 'independent' Love Jihadis—those who are not guided by any spirit, organisation, leader or religious agenda, but only by the passion and warmth in their hearts for another person. That will be genuine love, and a fitting reply to all Jihad and forms of hatred.

Ghalib's Poetic Beloved

Cruel, Willful, and Elusive

MEHR AFSHAN FAROOQI

Neend uski hai dimagh uska hai raten uski hain
teri zulfen jiske shanon par parishan ho gayen

Sleep is his, the mind is his, and the night is his
On whose shoulders your tresses are carelessly draped

The ghazal has always been associated with love. Indeed, in its early development in Arabia, it was the popular form used by Bedouin poets to express their feelings of loneliness and passion. It was usually a prelude to the ode or *qasidah*. Although the literary tradition of the ghazal can be traced to the Abbasids' court and its most famous poet Abu Nuvas (d.814), the blossoming of the ghazal in its complex, mystical form happened in Persia in the tenth century.[112] In the centuries that followed, the ghazal developed a distinctive array of themes, metaphors and technique. The Urdu ghazal that emerged from the Persian evolved by adapting and adopting local colors, vocabulary, cultural aesthetics and crafting metaphors that were suited to its poetic environment.

Much of Asadullah Khan Ghalib's (1797-1869) early Urdu poetry was marked by a distinct tilt towards Persian language idioms and imagery. It reveals a love for, and mastery of, arcane Persian, unmatched in any other poet before or after him. Yet, his love for abstract thought and his metaphorical reach to remote themes and ideas is a peculiarly Indian characteristic. Some Indian Persian writers developed this particular style of abstraction, known as *khiyalbandi*, in the seventeenth century, which literally means capturing a thought and rendering it into elegant verse.[113] *Khiyalbandi* reached its zenith in the poetry of the Indian Persian mystic poet Mirza Abdul Qadir Bedil (1644-1720). Ghalib was inordinately influenced by Mirza Bedil and other *khiyalband* poets. He may have felt that native Urdu words were not effective in dealing with the abstract, subtle and rare themes of *khiyalbandi*, many of which are based on fine distinctions in the way ideas are enunciated. Superficially his Urdu poetry, and certainly early Urdu poetry, sounds like Persian conscripted to appear under the guise of Urdu. But the spirit of that poetry is so utterly Indian that it cannot be classified as anything but Indian.

The seepage of Indian themes in Ghalib's poetry is evident in two broad, congruent areas: his approach to that big question of Creation, Creator and mankind; and the cultural aesthetic and worldview that he possesses from being an Indian Muslim, albeit of Turkish descent. I will first discuss, with a few quotes from Ghalib's early Urdu poetry, the cultural aesthetic as evident in the characteristics of the beloved.

In the following verse, Ghalib speaks of a dark-complexioned beloved who is nonetheless as admirably cruel, coquettish (*zalim*), and even more tantalizing than the conventional light-skinned beauty.

Rach gaya josh-e safa se zulf ka a'za men aks
hai nazakat jalvah ai zalim siyah famii teri

Your body's intense whiteness absorbed colour from
your tresses
O cruel beloved, the blackness of your complexion,
Exudes radiance of your delicateness

The theme of the dark-skinned beloved is not unknown in Urdu, but it has been reformulated here with typical Ghalibian flair and a unique *ta'lil.*[114] The white-to-blackness of the beloved has been given a delightful justification: She is extremely delicate, her long hair is dark and dense, and so her fair body reflects and absorbs the blackness of the tresses. The poet suggests that the *josh* or the fervor of her whiteness caused it to absorb the dark colour from her hair. *Josh* generally means 'passion', but it also means excess and a state of denseness caused by a crowd. Hence *josh* can also be interpreted as excessiveness, multitude, and extravagant abundance. *Josh* contains the implicit image of dyeing, which involves hot, bubbling colour, suggesting the verb *josh dena*, to boil, to excite. Note here the clever use of the verb *rachna*, which means 'something becoming so fully absorbed as to give its own colour to the object on which it has been applied.' Also, Ghalib speaks of *aks*; here it means reflection, and thus there is the hint of illusion. She may not have actually become dark but she appears to be so. Usually one associates *jalvah* or radiance with light. The radiance or glow of a dark complexion is alluded to in the second line. The radiance of *siyah fami*, says Ghalib, has a special aura of *nazakat* (delicateness).

The most striking vocabulary in this context of the beloved is *zalim.* Although it is originally an Arabic word, and used frequently in Persian, *zalim* does not have the praise-admiration sense in Persian; this sense is an invention of Urdu speakers.[115] Culturally, the Urdu milieu sees beauty as *zalim*. Another point to note here is that the darker complexion is presented as more enticing, more truly 'beautiful'.[116]

My second example of a dark-complexioned beloved builds on a cultural practice that is very Indian but couched in esoteric Sufic Persianisms.

Kasrat-e josh-e suvaida se nahin til ki jagah
khaal kab mashshatah de sakti hai kakul ke tale

The intensity of blackness has left no scope for the beauty mark
How can the bride/dancer apply the black dot beneath her curly hair?

A little black spot, usually made with *kajal,* is applied above the temple just below the hairline to ward off the 'evil eye'. But the beautiful dancer is so dark that the mark or *til* won't show. The verse has a charming ambiguity that has left open several possibilities of interpretation. Gyan Chand Jain in his commentary on Ghalib's excluded verses prefers to read *suvaida* as a black dot on the heart which, in Sufi parlance, is supposed to be the concentration point for God's true radiance (if the seeker can reach a certain level of knowledge). He interprets the verse as follows: Innumerable hearts are snared in the beloved's hair. Their *suvaidas* have left no room for a beauty mark.[117] Reading *suvaida* as the black dot on the heart can yield yet another interpretation: The beloved is so pure of heart that her *suvaida*, normally a nearly invisible spot in the heart, has overtaken her whole body, and that is why she is dark-complexioned. This interpretation lends a charming, romantic twist to a Sufi concept.

The ghazal from which this verse has been extracted has an extremely Indian (or indigenous) mood enhanced by the rustic *radif ke tale*. The word *tale* (beneath, below) is derived from the Sanskrit *tal*. The opening verse of this ghazal has a tantalizing image of the beloved bathing with rose water among roses in the garden:

Voh naha kar aab-e gul se saayah-e gul ke tale
baal kis garmii se sukhlata hai sumbul ke tale

After bathing in rose water beneath the roses
With what fervor does she dry her hair in the shade of
the hyacinth!

A woman, bathing in the open, in a garden under the shade of roses, and then drying her hair with fervent ardour, among the flower bushes and shrubs, these are very much Indic images and ideas. In fact, the theme of the beloved bathing in the open—in the river, or on the river bank—is a not a theme found in Persian, but has been extremely popular with Urdu poets from the seventeenth century. Here are two examples from the great eighteenth century poets Mir Taqi Mir and Ghulam Hamadani Musahafi.

Mir:

Shab nahata tha jo voh rashk-e qamar paani men
guthi mahtab se uthti thi lahar paani men

Last night that envy of the moon was bathing in open
water,
She caused the waves to rise entwined with the
moonlight in the water

Saath is lutf ke deta tha dikhaai voh badan
jaise jhamke hai bara gauhar-e tar paani men

With such elegance was her body descried,
It was if a pearl of high lustre was glistening under water

Musahafi:

Jumna men kal naha kar jab usne baal bandhe
hum ne bhi apne ji men kya kya khiyaal bandhe

Yesterday, after bathing in the Jamuna she tied up her hair,
I can't say what thoughts I twined and intertwined in my head

Thus we see that young Ghalib was backed by a strong literary and aesthetic tradition when he talked of his beloved bathing in the dew, or in rose water in the open garden, even if Ghalib's verse does not reach the heights of Mir's artful incorporation of the effect of the moon on water in this instance. Musahafi's imagination builds on twining desire with long hair. Going back to Ghalib's verse, we can observe the delightful intermixing of tropes, Persian and Indic. *Sunbul* or hyacinth is a fragrant clustered flower made up of smaller blooms that have curly petals; it has been used in Persian poetry as a trope for beautiful curly hair and was appropriated in Urdu for the same effect. This is the Perso-Indic crossover I am referring to here. An Indian beauty bathes in the rose garden and dries her hair among the Persian hyacinths.

Note that Ghalib has used the masculine gender (*sulkhlata*) here, which I have translated as feminine, not just because of the convention of English poetry, but also because the beloved, whose bathing is the subject of this verse, is clearly feminine. Similarly, in Mir, the pronouns and verbs are all masculine but we clearly understand that it's a woman he's talking about. In Musahafi, the gender is omitted, but the sense of a woman is very strong. This convention—of hiding the gender of the beloved, or of implying or stating that s/he is masculine—is not Iranian, as most of us have been led to believe, especially since Altaf Husain Hali (1837-1914) wrote his extremely influential book—the first Urdu book on literary theory—*Muqaddama-e Sh'er o Sha'iri* in 1893. Persian has no genders, so it would be unfair to assert that just because there is occasional mention in Persian ghazals of beautiful boys as cup bearers or a young, handsome youth as beloved, the Iranian ghazal always has a male beloved. In fact, the convention of talking of the beloved as male is a mode, inaugurated, strengthened and established by the Urdu poets of the early eighteenth century.[118] But for a couple of poets like Mubarak Abru (1683/5-1733) and Shakir Naji (c.1690-1744-47) who openly indulged their boy love in their poetry, it is not possible to name any Urdu poet from late seventeenth century Delhi who really *meant* the beloved to be a boy. In fact, the concept of the beloved in the Urdu ghazal very soon took on an abstract character—it was the *idea* of a beloved, and the *idea* of a lover, rather than an actual person. This could have been an influence of Sanskrit, from where those early Urdu poets of Delhi were also supposed to have derived their love for *sleṣa* that took the form of *iham* (wordplay, double entendre) in the ghazal of early eighteenth century Urdu poets. These subjects—the source for the love of *iham*, and love and lover as *ideas* rather than persons—have not been investigated, mainly because modern literary theory in Urdu chose to take a literalist view of all things pre-modern.[119]

Moving on from the beloved to the lover, Ghalib has a searing verse on the theme of burning in love, with a stunning image taken from Diwali, the Hindu festival of lights:

Hai tamasha gaah-e soz-e tazah har yak 'uzv-e tan
jun chiraghan-e diwali saf ba saf jalta hun main

Every limb of my body presents the spectacle of new fire
caused by her coquetry
Like the lamps of Diwali I burn row upon row

Comparing the body as burning spectacle (*chiraghan)* with Diwali lamps is an original idea, a marvel of metaphorical thinking. One of Ghalib's commentators, Zamin Kantoori, has suggested that the construction *chiraghan-e divali* is odd, because Ghalib has used a Persian *izafat* with an Indic word. I think the usage is notable for two reasons: one, because Ghalib here sets a precedent—or at least an authoritative instance—of such an *izafat* which is still frowned upon by the 'purists', and, two, he preferred to use a native image instead of a Perso-Arabic one.

Ghalib has a formidable reputation of being a cerebral poet, who deliberately seeks to complicate themes with far-fetched metaphor. This is true; yet, Ghalib has given us some of the most achingly beautiful verses that capture desire in so many colours. Every verse in the following ghazal, composed around 1821-26 by the young Ghalib, invokes longing for the beloved. It is Ghalib's longest, comprising 17 verses. It was also his favourite because he kept it in its entirety, not pruning a single verse. I am quoting a sample of four lines here to illustrate Ghalib's mastery in evoking emotion:

Muddat hui hai yaar ko mehman kiye hue
josh-e qadah se bazm chiraghan kiye hue

It's been ages since my friend was my guest
The effervescence of wine lit up the gathering

Dhunde hai phir kisi ko lab-e baam par havas
zulf-e siyah rukh pe pareshan kiye hue

Desire again searches for someone on the terrace lip
Dark tresses carelessly flowing over her face

Chahe hai phir kisi ko muqabil men aarzu
surmah se tez dushnah-e mizhgan kiye hue

Longing once more wants someone face to face
Her eyelash daggers sharpened with antimony

Iknun bahar-e naaz ko taake hai phir nigaah
samaan-e sad hazaar gulistan kiye hue

Once more the gaze gapes at the newly blossomed beauty
With a hundred gardens all arranged

Ji dhundhta hai phir wahi fursat ke raat din
baithe rahe tasavvur-e janan kiye hue

The heart searches for that leisure, when days and nights
Were spent thinking of the loved one

Ghalib's love poetry has a different tilt in *muamilah bandi* (conversation with the beloved) than his contemporary Momin Khan Momin or the great Mir Taqi Mir.

His lover, for example, can be more assertive and individualistic:

Voh apni khu na chchorenge hum apni vaza' kyun badlen
subuk sar ho keh kyun puchchen tum hum se sargaran kyun ho

He/she won't change her habits, why should I change my ways
Why should I be anxious and ask, 'Are you upset with me.'

Vaan yeh ghuroor-o naaz yan yeh hijaab-e paas-e vaz'
raah men hum milen kahaan bazm men voh bulaae kyun

There her arrogance in glorious coquetry, here our concern for decorum
Where would we meet on the wayside, why should she invite us to her revelry?

Here it must be emphasized that the ghazal is not a typical 'love poem' or a lyric but an engagement with the idea of love and loving. The genderless beloved can therefore either be human, god, or any other creature. The ghazal transcends time because it has a tropic universe of its own, lifting love to dizzy heights of passion by creating a beloved who is intensely desirable but almost unattainable. This beloved possesses characteristics that are extreme, and in fact can seem strange outside of the poetics of the ghazal. For example, the beloved is exaggeratedly haughty, cruel, tall, slender and beautiful. Her eyebrows are curved like daggers, eyelashes long and sharp as needles, waist thin as a strand of hair, and hair dark as night. The beloved inflicts wounds that never heal. Nonetheless, it is possible to relate to, and identify with, the lover and beloved because the emotions invoked are universal. A nuanced, careful reading can help us understand how each poet carves or develops tropes to produce individualized depictions of even the most common themes. The experience of love, however much stylized or couched in metaphor, does allow great poets to attain imaginative flights through language. Urdu poets stretch language to its limits to encompass dimensions ranging from self-mockery and despair to delight in body and spirit of existence. A successful verse is unsentimental, yet a powerful and emotional expression that is not narrowly personal, but strikes an empathetic chord in the listener or reader.

Because love is an idea, it blossoms in the world of the poet's imagination. As an idea, it is free and fluid, not pinned down by reality's strictures. The lover-beloved in the ghazal can be worldly, that is, the emotions expressed are directed towards an earthly beloved, *ishq-e majazi* or, they could represent a higher, sublime level of devotion, such as love for God, *ishq-e haqiqi*. The love for an earthly creature is *majazi*, that is, metaphorical, while love for God is *haqiqi*, or real, the beauty of this arrangement being that the metaphorical can be a simulation of the real, one leading to the other. This also explains Ghalib's engagement with philosophical questions that are central to ghazal poetry, namely: What is the meaning of Creation? What is humankind's relation with God and place in Creation? What, then, is the deeper meaning of love?

Since the lover's fate is to suffer, and the beloved's is to inflict suffering, pain and all that causes pain thus have a positive value. This positive equation of love and pain is the source of many images and metaphors in the Urdu ghazal. The beloved may be cruel either out of indifference or to test the lover's perseverance, but the lover-protagonist prefers death at the hands of the beloved to indifference. Within this stylized, self-contained universe of ghazal poetry, love is therefore the basis of an elaborate range of emotions, including pain. The experience of love involves wounding, an opening and softening of the heart, which then prepares it for higher, perhaps more profound states of love.

Love, Society, Polity

Urdu Poetry from Khusro to Faiz

ZAFAR ANJUM

I recently gave a talk on eminent poet and philosopher Dr Muhammad Iqbal in Singapore. Many in the audience had not heard much about Dr Iqbal. Some of them, however, had heard of Mirza Ghalib. After the talk was over, a lady asked me privately: Did Iqbal compose poetry on love like Ghalib? It was an innocent question but it betrayed the popular perception of Urdu poetry—that it is the poetry of love, and that Ghalib is its main composer. But this is not the case. Apart from Ghalib, Mir, Momin, Jigar, Daagh, and Faiz, there have been many greats in Urdu who have imbued its poetry with a romantic flavour. Urdu poets have offered love the highest possible pedestal in the hierarchy of subjects, and have celebrated its myriad colours and dimensions with great ardour, passion and thoughtfulness.

At the same time, there have been major literary savants including Altaf Hussain Hali, Akbar Allahabadi, Maulana Hasrat Mohani and Allama Iqbal who have gone beyond matters of love and tackled many complex themes and dimensions of life such as empire, nation and nationhood,

Sufism, and the encroachment of modernity into our lives—issues that have dominated the thoughts and concerns of Indian communities in the last few centuries. Going beyond Ghalib, this essay pays homage to the oeuvres of many other Urdu poets from Amir Khusro to Faiz Ahmed Faiz. Rather than focus only on romantic love, it also explores complex social and political themes, and their treatment in Urdu poetry.[120]

To begin tracing the deep links between Urdu poetry and love, it must first be noted that Urdu poetry has several forms: *nazm, ghazal, qasida, masnavi* (or *mathnavi*), *marsia* and *rubai*. Among all these forms, ghazal (a genre of lyric poem, generally short and graceful in form and typically dealing with themes of love) remains one of the most popular genres. The literal meaning of ghazal is talking to women about love or 'the talk of boys and girls'.[121] As such, this form of poetry is most suitable to give vent to a lover's anguish, longing, and ecstasy. Its canvas is broad and it can bear on its shoulders expression of all kinds of romantic and non-romantic emotions and sentiments.

Ghazal, which originated in Arabia in the late seventh century, later travelled to Persia and much of central Asia. The predecessors of the Delhi sultanate brought it to India around the eleventh century. Although in its existing mode, the ghazal has been written by poets as a form of personal expression, at most to be recited in gatherings such as *mushairas* (poetic soirees), it may originally have had a folk, celebratory nature, to be sung in public, with lute-like instruments. In any case, it is a popular mode of melodic expression and has found audiences in every age, proving not only the versatility of this genre, but also its ability to relate to every generation.

Love, of course, is not only romantic. The first expression of love in Urdu (or Hindvi) poetry was Sufi or mystical love. Amir Khusro (1253-1325), the legendary court poet who served as many as seven Delhi rulers, wrote ghazals and *mathnavis* (long panegyric poems) for his patrons, and composed tunes for his ghazals by incorporating Persian and Indian musical styles. For one sultan, Mu'iz-ud-Din Kaiqubad, Khusro would compose a new ghazal everyday, to be sung by one 'Turmati Khatoon, whose voice would reach the sky'.[122] The Sufi monasteries were another platform where ghazal was used to enhance the mystics' spiritual states—again accompanied mostly by Indian instruments. These two traditions are often considered the precursors of the present-day ghazal gaeki (ghazal singing style), the qawwali, and some other classical forms of North Indian music. While almost all ghazal poets in India till the thirteenth or fourteenth century wrote in the Persian language, Khusro may be one of the first to have also used Hindvi (ancestor to the modern Hindi/Urdu) or sometimes a mixture of Hindvi and Persian. For example, the famous ghazal '*Ze Hale Miskin Makun Taghaful...*' ('Do not overlook my misery...') is ascribed to him. But the first authentic poets to have used an Indian language to compose ghazals are Quli Qutub Shah and Wali of the Deccan. Urdu may have originated in North India, but it flourished when it travelled to the South and found loving hosts in the courts of Golconda and Bijapur.

Qutub Shah, who ruled for 31 years between 1580 and 1611, favoured simplicity of style and was very fond of beauty in nature. Being a king, his was a life of luxury; and so we do not find even a shade of melancholia in his oeuvre. His beloved was present by his side, so he did not have to evoke an imaginary lover in his poetic world. In Qutub Shah's palace, dance parties were organized where the king's compositions were sung. His poetic themes included beauties of the palace, festivals, elephants, and even horses. Although his poetry is bereft of grief, the following ghazal became quite famous, as he composed it out of sadness when he failed to see his real-life beloved once or twice:

Piya baaj piyala piya jaye na
Piya baaj ek til jiya jaye na
Kahete piya bin saboori karoon
Kahiya jaye amma kiya jaye na
Nahin ishq jis wo bada kodh hai
Kahin us se mil baisiya jaye na
Qutub Shah ne de mujh diwane ko pand
Diwane ko kuchh pand diya jaye na!

I can't sip from the wine-cup without my beloved,
I can't live without her even for a moment,
I'm advised that I should be patient,
When my beloved is not around,
It's easier said than done.
A man who is not in love is a waste,
How can one tolerate such a man's company?
O Qutub Shah! Don't counsel a zany fellow like me!
For a mad man can scarcely be counseled.[123]

Wali Dakkani (1667-1707), on the other hand, addressed moral issues and talked about the ethical conduct of people in his ghazals, which had so far been limited to conversations with women. In his poetry, his beloved takes many forms: sun, fire, mirror and light. In the following couplet, the poet invokes the sun as a simile:

Mukh tera aftaab mehshar hai
Noor uska jahaan mein ghar bhar hai

The beloved's face is as bright as the sun,
Its radiance has spread to each and every house in the world.

By comparing his beloved's face to the sun, Wali implies that she is also as popular as the sun, and that he can see her everywhere. He says in further appreciation of his beloved:

Chahta hai is jahan mein gar bahisht
Ja tamash dekh us rukhsaar ka
Yaad karna har ghadi us yaar ka
Hai wazifa mujh dil-e beemaar ka

If you desire to dwell in paradise in this world
Go and watch the frolics of that beauty
Remembrance of that beloved, every moment
ensures the subsistence of this sick heart.

For Wali, his beloved is as pretty as the much-desired houris of paradise, and her face is paradise on earth. For him, remembering his beloved is a prayer, a chant that heals his sickened heart, a heart afflicted with love.

By the seventeenth century, the northern and southern traditions of ghazal merged. In the following two centuries, this form of poetry really blossomed in Delhi and Lucknow—the two schools of Urdu poetry. Many Sufi poets further enriched the sensual and erotic background of the ghazal. Ghazals were formally recited at mushairas, where many poets recited their compositions to an applauding audience.

As the sun began to set on the Mughal empire and a new power, Great Britain, was gaining ascendance in

India through the East India Company, the vast country got divided into a number of smaller states. At that point of time, the nobility in India wallowed in social and moral decadence, given to a life of extravagance and ostentation. As this class became meaningless and cut off from reality, poets began to portray an ideal life in their compositions; this was their escape into fantasy.

In this age, the portrayal of love transcended the bounds of spirituality and focused on physicality—bodily love. Epicurean pursuits became dominant and Allah's *ibadat* (praying to God) was confined to decoration of graves and celebration of *Urs*. This was love in the age of Empire.

Against this political and social backdrop, Mirza Mohammad Rafi Sauda (born in Delhi in 1713), who often infused his poetry with humour, challenged even Majnoo, the legendary lover and perhaps India's equivalent of Romeo:

Sambhal ke rakhiyo qadam rah-e ishq me majnoo
Ke is nawah me Sauda barahna pa bhi hai

Majnoo, supposedly the greatest of all lovers, had left his home for the sake of love and endured the harshness of the jungle and the desert. Sauda cautions him before he sets his foot in the lane of love, saying that he has a competitor; the barefoot Sauda is already there. Further, his humourous temperament makes him say this about his beloved:

Kaifiyat-e chashm uski mujhe yaad hai Sauda
Saaghar ko mere haath se lena ke 'chala main'

Emblazoned on my memory is the state of my beloved's eyes
Take away the goblet from me, here I depart.

Vividly remembering the look in the eyes of his beloved, he says he is going back or leaving this world altogether. Speaking of Allah's *ibadat*, then, Sauda implies that for a lover, the heart is more sacred than the Ka'aba—the House of God in Mecca:

Ka'aba agarche tuta to kya ja-ye gham hai sheikh
Yeh qasar-e dil nahin ke banaya na jayega

If the Ka'aba (a sacred place) is destroyed, is it a matter of much gloom?
It is not the palace of the heart that it could not be rebuilt!

One of the most common ways to describe a lover and a beloved in Urdu poetry is through the imagery of the moth and the candle. Innumerable couplets have been composed around this imagery over centuries. This is how Sauda tries his hand at this:

Aye jo bazm mei to utha chehre se naqaab
Parwane ko hi shamma se bezaar kar chale

When you have come to the gathering, take off your veil
Why make the moth indifferent to the candle!

When Mir Taqi Mir (1723–1810) and Khwaja Mir Dard (1721–1785) arrived on the scene, their voices articulated the anxiety, depression, and pessimism of their age. Mir's concept of love mixed the traditional concept of death with his idea of love. Mir thought it idealistic to lay down one's life for a cause. However, Dard believed that complete drowning of oneself is possible only with God. In Urdu ghazals, Dard's verses are full of love for God, without relinquishing lyricism:

Jag me aa kar idhar udhar dekha
Tu hi aaya nazar jidhar dekha

Coming into this world, I saw here and there
Wherever I saw, I saw only you.

Mir witnessed the disintegration of the mighty Mughal empire. His poetry, therefore, echoed the voice of that period's suffering souls, offering a positive face to feelings of despondency and gloom. This made his poetry heart-rending and equipped the reader with a new consciousness of life and the universe. Owing to his masterful hold over the medium, Mir is called the king of ghazal. Look at the kind of lover he envisions:

Hoga kisi deewar ke saaye me khada Mir
Kya kaam mohabbat se us aaraamtalab ko

Mir must be standing by a wall's shadow
Why would that waster bother himself with love?

In this couplet, the word '*aaraamtalab*' (waster or self-indulgent) connotes a special meaning. A failed lover, leaving behind his home and all its comforts, stands by the wall of his beloved's house. He is being accused of being lazy, a person given to luxury; and what does such a person have to do with love? If this is being lazy and luxury seeking, then what is love? What is the pain of love? What does the poet expect of the lover?

The answers to at least some of these questions point to how love, for Mir, is as much pain as pleasure, a consciousness of life that is not entirely separate from death. Reading some of his couplets gives us the impression of looking at a painting:

Nazuki us ke lab ki kya kahiye
Pankhudi ek gulab ki si hai

How can one describe how delicate her lips are,
As if they were a rose petal.

Mir praises the lips (of his beloved) because he sees life in them. He wants to admire them but does not find adequate words to express his feelings. He runs his mind over many choices and finally finds the petal of a rose worth comparing to the lips of his beloved: the rose petal, just blossomed out of a bud, is full of delicate beauty and colour. It looks fresh and full of life. He likens it to a flower's petal; nevertheless, he is not satisfied even with this epithet as it can hardly do justice to the beauty of the beloved's lips.

Mir has created more impact using '*ki*', '*si*' and '*sa*' than by his similes and epithets.

Dekh to dil ki jaan se uthta hai
Yeh dhuan sa kahan se uthta hai

See, the heart is growing weary of life,
Where does this smoke-like thing come from?

Here the lover is dying, love having shaken his whole entity. By saying, 'smoke-like', and using an interrogative style, Mir has tried to differentiate between the smoke that is caused by the burning of wood and coal and that caused by love's depression and gloom, because woodsmoke will vanish after some time but the smoke arising from heartburn will leave its impact.

Yun uthe aah us gali se hum
Jaise koi jahan se uthta hai

I lifted myself up from that street,
As if someone leaves for the heavenly abode.

In contrast to Mir's pessimism, Daagh (born in Delhi in 1831), who found solace and comfort as the Nizam's court poet in Hyderabad, was full of easy banter that is very much reflected in his poetry:

Gulshan me tere labon ne goya
Ras choos liya kali kali ka

In the garden, your lips have, as if,
Sucked the nectar out of each bud.

In keeping with the thematic and other shifts in Urdu poetry, the foundations of love in Daagh's compositions are material and materialistic. His beloved is not some unimaginable power but a mortal human being in and of this world. Daagh's lover is a successful lover. His poetry is full of joyous rendition, with feelings being clearly expressed. In the following couplet, Daagh competes with his beloved in a unique way:

Mashooq se bhi hum ne nibhayi barabari
Waan lutf kam hua to yahan pyar kam hua

With the beloved I practised a measure of equality,
She reduced her blessings, I reduced my love.

Dagh even treated *mehshar* (Resurrection or Day of Judgment) in a humourous vein:

Mehshar me khalq apni musibat me mubtala
Yaan yeh talaash aaye koi khoob-roo pasand

On the Day of Judgment, everyone is worried for himself,
While my worry is finding a beauty of my choice.

Mehshar me baad purshish ahwaal dekhna
Hum dekhte phirenge tamaasha idhar udhar

On the Day of Judgment, after the accounts are done,
I'll be busy eyeing the spectacle here and there.

Raqibon ke hathon se mehshar ke din
Tumhein chheen kar main agar le gaya?

From the clutches of my rivals, on the Day of Judgment,
What if I were to snatch you away?

Maza ho hash'r me dono hon ek saath talab
Hamare saath chalo saamne khuda ke tum

Delight me it will, were both of us called together on the Day of Judgment,
Along with me you go before the Almighty,

Dil ka aana hai kaam se jaana
Jaayega kaam se to ayega

Falling in love is akin to losing one's life,
Losing life is of some use, then.

Between Mir and Daagh's time was the age of Mirza Ghalib (born in 1797 in Agra). As mentioned earlier, he was arguably the most popular Urdu poet ever; and while this essay does not focus on his work, it is important to at least mention his immense contribution. Ghalib sometimes adopted a simple lyrical diction like that of Mir, but oftentimes his compositions were complicated due to heavy Persianization. However, when it comes to the poetry of love, Ghalib's virtuosity remains unmatched, probably with the exception of Mir. Look at the simplicity of this verse:

Ishq ne Ghalib nikamma kar diya
Warna hum bhi aadmi the kaam ke

Love has rendered me useless,
Else, I too was a diligent worker!

Or this, a cautious note on love:

Yeh ishq nahin asaan bus itna samajh lijie
Ek aag ka dariya hai aur doob ke jana hai

Love is not easy an affliction, do you understand?
It is a river of fire, and one can only cross it by drowning in it.

By the end of the nineteenth century, as India's struggle for free nationhood slowly took shape, we begin to witness another type of love—love for the nation, an important development in the age of Empire.

Syed Fazal-ul Hasan Hasrat (born in 1857 in a village called Mohaan in Unnau district of Uttar Pradesh) was interested in politics right from his student days. After his BA, he launched a literary and political paper titled *Urdu-e Mualla*. In that magazine, he wrote an essay on the policies of the British, and consequently was imprisoned, with hard labour, for a year and a half. He was a simple, sincere, and fearless man who spent his life in abject penury, and this also affected his poetry. Because of this, though his poetry has colour and youthfulness, its tone is always despairing.

The main point to note is that he was the only flag bearer of ancient lyricism in the modern age. Also, he had a clear understanding of the emotions and sentiments of young boys and girls living in the environment of Muslim joint families, and gave voice to their emotions in a beautiful and unhindered fashion, which is unprecedented. What follows is a famous ghazal, very popular among singers:

Chupke chupke raat din aansoo bahana yaad hai
Hum ko ab tak aashiqi ka wo zamana yaad hai
Ba hazaraan izteraab o sad hazaaran ishtiyaaq

Tujh se wo pehle pahal dil ka lagaanaa yaad hai
Kheench lena wo mera parde ka kona daf'atan
Aur dupatte se tera munh ka chipana yaad hai
Tujh se milte hi wo kuchh bebaak ho jana mera
Aur tera daantoon me wo ungali dabaana yaad hai

I remember those silent sessions of crying day and night,
I still remember those days of our torrid love affair.
With thousands of perturbed emotions and profound eagerness,
I remember the first moment of falling in love with you.
I remember how I had twitched the corner of your veil,
I remember how you quickly hid your face behind the mantle.
I remember those bold advances I used to make when we met,
I remember how you used to put your finger between your teeth.

However, the most famous Urdu poet who wrote patriotic poems was Dr. Muhammad Iqbal (1878-1938).

Iqbal, often referred to as the spiritual father of Pakistan, started out as an Indian nationalist. Following the footsteps of Akbar Allahabadi, he celebrated India's multiculturalism, called Lord Ram 'Imam-e Hind', and India the land of Chisti and Nanak. He wrote paeans to its eternal beauty, the most famous being his nazm, 'Saare Jahan Se Achha Hindoositan Hamara' which became immensely popular, and is sung till today as India's second national anthem. Iqbal spent three years in Europe, pursing higher education in Cambridge and Munich, and that phase transformed his outlook—the spirit of Islam seeped into his soul, and changed him forever.[124]

Iqbal, in his poetry, celebrated dynamism and action. He was a poet who sought to inspire the love of '*amal*' (action) in human beings. Even though he was critical of the materialism of the West, he admired its dynamism. He often intermixed that dynamic aspect of human nature with Oriental or even Islamic motifs:

> *Be-khatar kood pada aatish-e namrood me ishq*
> *Aql hai mahwe tamasha-e lab-e baam abhi*
>
> Love jumped fearlessly into the bonfire lit by Nimrod,
> But the (calculating) intellect is still watching the show from the housetop.[125]

Ishq, love in the sense of devotion to a cause (for example, a noble scientist being devoted to fighting a deadly disease and finding a cure for it), is one of the most decisive factors in shaping a human's destiny—and in turn, shaping the destiny of a community or nation:

> *Agar hai ishq to hai kufr bhi musalmani*
> *Na ho mard-e musalman bhi kafir o zandiq*
>
> Given 'ishq' even denial is Islam
> Without it a Muslim is no better than an atheist and an unbeliever.[126]

The last great Urdu poet, in the tradition of Ghalib and Iqbal, was Faiz Ahmad Faiz (born in 1911 in Sialkot). Faiz joined the Progressive Writers' Association in 1936, and his participation in the labour movement provided depth to his thoughts. *Gham-e jana* (Sorrow of the beloved) and *gham-e rozgar* (Sorrow of earning one's keep, arising out of the pain/worries caused by the extraction of labour in pursuit of economic activities) took the shape of *gham-e watan* (Sorrow/worries for the beloved nation) and *gham-e jahan* (Sorrow of the world or worldly concerns). When Pakistan was created after dividing India, his dream was broken. He did not get the independence that he had desired. '*Subah-e Aazadi*' portrays that pain:

Yeh daagh daagh ujala yeh shabgazida sahar
Woh intezaar tha jiska yeh woh sahar to nahin
Yeh woh sahar to nahin jiski aarzo lekar
Chale the yaar ke mil jayegi kahin na kahin...

This stain-covered daylight, this night-bitten sunrise,
This is not that dawn that we had waited for;
This is not that dawn in quest of which,
Friends had set out, with hope in their hearts.

The tragedy of modern man is that he is torn between the demands of love and that of earning a livelihood. Faiz beautifully captures this dichotomy in the following composition:

Woh log bahut khush-qismat the
Jo ishq ko kaam samajhte the
Hum jeete ji masroof rahe
Kuchch ishq kiya kuchch kaam kiya
Kaam ishq ke aade aata raha
Aur ishq se kaam ulajhta raha
Phir aakhir tang aakar hum ne
Dono ko adhura chhod diya

Those were very fortunate people,
Who pursued love like a profession.
I remained busy throughout life,
Pursuing both love and work.
Work hindered love,
Love got entangled with work,
Tiring of this dichotomy,
I left both of them half-done.

For Faiz, poetry's canvas is broad enough to accommodate the pain and woes of humanity and human brotherhood, which were akin to his own afflictions. He said:

Duniya ne teri yaad se begana kar diya
Tujh se bhi dil fareb hain gham rozgar ke

The world has kept me at a distance from your memory,
Troubles of the world were more fascinating than you.

From the time of Amir Khusro to the age of Faiz, the expression of love has thus come a long way in Urdu poetry. For Faiz, fashioning a politically just society is ultimately more important than fulfilling the demands of a lover. He says:

Mujh se pehli si mohabbat mere mahboob na maang

Don't ask of me the love I earlier had for you, my love

And

Aur bhi gham hain zamane me muhabbat ke siwa
Rahanten aur bhi hain wasl ki rahat ke siwa

There are other sorrows too, besides the sorrows of love,
There are other comforts too, besides the comfort of a congress.

In summary, love has been one of the most dominant themes in Urdu poetry, even as the many ideas of love and its complex relationships with society and polity have undergone sometimes subtle and at other times drastic shifts. Unfortunately, the language itself is going into a decline. The only consolation is that, thankfully, the great Urdu poets of yore have left for us one of the richest treasures of love poetry.

Barahmasa

Songs for the Seasons of Love and Separation

RAKHSHANDA JALIL

The *barahmasas*, meaning songs for the twelve months of the year according to the Indian lunar calendar, are songs of separation—both mystic and secular—expressing love and longing for the beloved. The singer's mood changes with the seasons and thus allows the poet to incorporate local, seasonal and natural elements while essentially drawing upon a single theme: love, or rather, meeting (*milna*) and its conjoined twin *bichhadna* (separation). Drawing upon its ancient roots in Prakrit, Sanskrit, Hindi and regional dialects, the *barahmasa* is almost entirely rural. It still survives in the form of *lok geet* or folk songs. Or, looked at another way, one can say that the *barahmasa* draws upon *lok geet* and existing oral traditions, and gives them a more seasonal colour.

The past and the present fuse in the *barahmasa* as the poet draws upon the popular Hindavi tradition of *virah* or separation and creates a landscape in which there is no reality save the anguished yearning of the *virahini*, or a woman who lives in a state of perpetual separation from her beloved. It is this anguish that gets recorded month after month in plaintive, plentiful detail. One might well ask: Why should a woman's longing for her absent lover hold any especial interest? What merit is to be found in these works—almost all being little other than variations on a single theme, all using the same stock of images, metaphors and conceits? Especially, since many are by lesser-known poets and some by virtually unknown composers? Despite its limitations and 'lack' of refinements, I do believe the *barahmasa* deserves to be studied for several reasons that I shall enumerate.

Sometimes taking the colour of a *lok geet*, sometimes adopting the tone of a *qissa-kahani*, the *barahmasa* drew inspiration from a variety of sources: the Jain narrative poems describing Neminath's desertion of his wife Rajmati on their wedding day; a swathe of devotional poetry that dwelt on Radha's longing for Krishna; the description of the seasons in Kalidas's epic poem *Ritu Samhar* (literally meaning a compilation of the six seasons) that, in turn, spawned a tradition of *rituvarnan* (poetic description of the seasons); elements of *singhar rasa* (the *rasa* or 'flavour' of erotica, one of the nine *rasas*) that have influenced the depiction of the *nayika* (the 'heroine' or female protagonist) both in verse and painting; an accumulated stock of similes and metaphors that had gained currency largely through word of mouth. Drawing upon these diverse sources, appropriating easily understood stock images and speaking in a woman's voice, the *barahmasa* allowed the fullest possible exploration of the link between memory and desire. It used the set format of the seasons—and the fairs, festivals, rites, customs, flora and fauna associated with the twelve months of the year that are constant and therefore predictable—to reinforce the near-universal experience of love and separation. And in a country such as India, with its largely agrarian society and an agricultural system based on the annual arrival of the Monsoons, the *barahmasa* acquires a special resonance.

But what sets apart the *barahmasa* from other forms of erotic or romantic poetry is the social commentary that leavens its description of love and longing. The *aap biti* (personal) becomes a *jag beeti* (collective) and the scenes of pastoral beauty become pages from a rural calendar as the description of rural life is spiked with lively observations about society. In the *Barahmasa Kanwal Dei*, for instance, written by the poet Johri from Bihar and quoted by Tanveer Alvi in *Urdu Mein Baramase ki Riwayat*, the trials and tribulations of the times find reflection too, much like the *shaher ashob* ('lament of the city') tradition of classical Urdu literature.[127] The poet Maqsood, who belonged to the *bhishti* (water-carrier) community in the Awadh region and was considered a *baazar* poet by the cognoscenti, paints realistic pictures of nature and society and studs his tale with the minutiae of small, everyday domestic life, routine seasonal tasks, mundane housekeeping details such as the repairs done to roofs, walls, fences and boundaries during the rains.[128] We find, therefore, a subaltern voice mingling with the *birah katha* ('tale of separation'), making a larger commentary about life.

A product of *qasbahs* and suburbs, the *barahmasas* were remarkably free of the courtly influences that characterized the rest of Urdu poetry, most notably the ghazal. Moreover, the *barahmasa* poets made a conscious effort to move away from the crippling influence of Persian that held sway over the court poets and displayed a remarkable readiness to experiment with other forms of poetic expression. Evidently, they reveled in the liberating air of dialects such as Braj-bhasha, Khari-boli, Awadhi, Rajasthani, and the occasional smattering of Dakhani just as much as they did in re-inventing or re-appropriating a literary space that had existed in the shade of the high form, be it the *riti* poetry in Hindi (traditionally written by court poets) or the ghazal and *masnavi* in Urdu.[129] The *barahmasa* then appears before us as a valuable testament to multiculturalism, multilingualism and multifariousness. They tell us that voices other than the male voice existed (even if the female voice was presented by a male composer and through a male perspective), that genres other than the classical were popular and that the Urdu poet showed a willingness to accommodate different poetic traditions.[130] More importantly, the *barahmasa* points to a time when Urdu had not established itself as a hegemonic force—in a literary and linguistic sense—nor acquired the purely urban/cosmopolitan consciousness it now displays.

Sometime in the early seventeenth century (1636 or so), Afzal Jhinjhanvi compiled the first *barahmasa* in Urdu and called it *Bikat Kahani* (*bikat* meaning 'immense' or 'terrible'). Here's a sampling:

Ari jab kook koel ne sunayi
Tamami tan badan mein aag lahi
Andher rain, jugnu jagmagata
Oo ka jalti upar tais ka jalata?

Ah, when the cuckoo sounds her cooing
It sets my body aflame
The glow worm glows in the darkness of the night
Why does it burn one already on fire?

And, elsewhere:

Gayi barsaat rut nikhara falak sab
Nami danam ke sajan ghar phire kab
Piya bin aikal kaise rahoo ri
Sitam upar sitam kaise sahoon ri

The rains are gone, the skies are clear
But I don't know when my beloved will return
How will I live alone without my beloved?
How will I bear affliction upon affliction?

The most-often quoted verses found in most *tazkiras*, however, remain the bitter-sweet lament:

Paden na mil mere peim phansi
Maran apna hai aur logon ko hansi

(Here I am with the noose of love around my neck
And people can only laugh at my plight.)

Close to Surdas's Braj-bhasha and Kabir's Sudakhahni, Afzal's Khari-boli had crossed the Jamuna and entered the Doaba region to drink deeply from both Braj-bhasha and Khari-boli. In fact, linguists such as Masood Husain Khan have studied the *barahmasas* as a barometer of the advance of Braj and Khari-boli into Urdu, the changing tone and tenor of *rekhta* and the extent of this intermingling over a period of roughly 350 years.[131] In literary terms, too, Afzal's *Bikat Kahani* is important because he introduced three basic elements that would remain the hallmark of the *barahmasa*: a *gharelu lehja* (domestic tone), *dramai tarz* (dramatic tone), and *khud-kalami* (use of first person).

We find the first mention of Afzal's *Bikat Kahani* in the *tazkira* of Sheikh Muhammad Qayamuddin Qayam's *Makhzan Nikaat* (written in 1755 or so), where Afzal is placed alongside Amir Khusro as a poet of the people. Afzal and his by now hugely popular epic poem also found mention in Mir Hasan's *tazkira Shoara-e-Urdu* (1778). Aloys Sprenger (1813-1893), the Austrian orientalist, preparing a catalogue of the library of the nawabs of Awadh in 1856, mentions *Bikat Kahani* and informs his readers that a copy of the said text is to be found in the India Office Library. However, *A Catalogue of Hindustani Manuscripts in the India Office Library, London* by B. Hardy, wrongly describes Afzal's poem thus: 'Bekat Kahani: a Bara Masa poem describing the grief of a woman separated from her lover at each month of the year by Gopal.'[132] This confusion is apparently created by the last verse in Afzal's poem, written in Persian:

Bayaad-e-dil ruba khush haal mi baash
Gahe Afzal gahe Gopal mi baash

According to Hashmi and Khan, 'Gopal' is the name Afzal took for himself during his stay in Mathura and indicates the extent and influence of Krishna *bhakti* on a wide swath of people regardless of the boundaries of faith or dialect. Such was the evident popularity of Afzal's poem that it not only spurred the composition of *barahmasas* but also spawned several titled, like his, '*Bikat Kahani*'. Afzal's *Bikat Kahani* continued to inspire generations of poets; almost two hundred years later, Abdullah Ansari writing his own *barahmasa* (in about 1823 or so), begins with a eulogy of the 'master':

Zanani boli hai uski pyari
Jise sun kar ho dil mein be-qarari

(His women's dialect is so lovely
That it causes a turbulence in the listener's heart.)

While Afzal's *Bikat Kahani* is mentioned in the *tazkira* by Mir Hasan, most other *barahmasas* have been kept beyond the pale. Little scholarly work has been done, even in Urdu, on the *barahmasa* tradition save for the compilation of twelve *barahmasas* by Tanveer Alvi. Alvi's book is important not merely because it places before the researcher a smorgasbord of delights (culled painstakingly from a variety of archival sources), but also because it shows the range of the genre—both geographical and linguistic. For instance, within the pages of Alvi's volume, one can find a variety of *barahmasas*: Uzlat from Gujarat, Johri from Bihar, Najeeb from Tonk in Rajasthan, Wahshat from Rampur, Hifzullah Qadiri from Badayun, Maqsood from Lucknow; one can also find Wahab writing in Bhojpuri, Ilahi Bakhsh and Abdullah Ansari in Khari-boli. Then there is Mir Abdul Wali Uzlat from Surat who travelled to Aurangabad and Delhi and picked up different folk elements along the way. Drawing on the existing *barahmasa* tradition in Gujarati, Uzlat incorporated literary devices such as the *kah mukarni* (a kind of riddle played between women that centres around denial), *do arthi* (double meaning), *shesh arthi* (six meaning), *kabad, dohra, chhand, surtha,* and *jhoolna*. He also broadened his frame of reference to include lovers from a variety of literary traditions, namely Laila-Majnu, Shashi-Punnu, Shirin-Farhad, Yusuf-Zulaikha, Heer-Ranjha, Gopi-Kanhaiya. Here's a sample of a *do arthi* couplet:

Papiha de namak ghaavon ko ke pee
Ghari sa har ghari doobe mera jee

(The cuckoo pours salt over my wounds and tells me to drink it
While all the while my heart sinks from minute to minute)

And another that shows Uzlat's use of an idiom that is spoken till this day:

> *Woh mehru bin jo kaatik maas aaya*
> *Palang pati se lag gayi sookh kaya*
>
> (The month of Kartik has come without bringing my beloved
> My emaciated body clings to the bed in longing)

A happy and eclectic mix-and-match remained the defining quality of the *barahmasa*. The *hudhud* (Arabic name for the hoopoe bird), which is mentioned in the Holy Quran as well as the legend of King Solomon and Queen Sheeba, appears in the story of Raja Ratan Kunwar and Sundarkali in the *Barahmasa Sundarkali* by an anonymous poet. The rustic maiden pining for her royal lover invokes both Khwaja Khizr and the village pundit in a wonderful display of syncretism and pluralism. Interspersed with descriptions of fairs and festivals, especially seasonal festivals which are common to all irrespective of faith or creed, the *barahmasas*, such as the one by Maqsood, depict the *nayika* going to pray at the shrine of a Sufi saint in her village or hamlet and—with much the same devotion—going to the village pundit for *faal nikalna*, i.e. the practice of opening the holy book to seek answers. In fact, several *barahmasas*, regardless of the faith of the composer, began with a *hamd* (an invocation to Allah), followed by a *naat* (panegyric in praise of the Prophet). Most had descriptions of Holi during *Phagun* and Diwali in the month of *Kartik*. Invariably, all began in the month of *Asaarh* (coinciding with June-July). And *all* spoke of a woman's body, its demands and longings, with unabashed details. The *virahini* of the *barahmasa*, for all her plaintiveness, is a far cry from the anemic, sexually indistinct beloved of the ghazal. She is full-bodied and red-blooded:

Woh joban hai ke jyu anaar ka phal
Bhari mithas se jyu misri ki jyu daal

(Her youth is like the pomegranate fruit
Bursting with sweetness like a lump of sugar)

The *virahini* feels the pain of separation most keenly in the month of *Saawan.* For it is during the rains that men traditionally stayed or returned home as business was slack, possibly because roads became un-passable. Tradition also demanded that a young bride would be called to her parents' home, when her brother would be sent to fetch her at the beginning of the season; shortly after a token visit, she would return to her husband's home and resume her conjugal life. When there is a departure from this time-honoured way of life, when she finds herself alone and bereft during the months of the rains (traditionally said to last for a *chaumasa*, or four months), then the dark clouds, the call of the *koel*, the darts of rain, the smell of damp earth, the dancing peacocks, the blood-red *birbahuti* insects, remind her that all other women are with their husbands while she is not. She is reminded of seasons past when she had enjoyed the plentiful rains with her beloved, and is tormented by the thought of his dalliances elsewhere. Hifzullah Qadiri has this to say about his *nayika* in his *Barahmasa Neha*:

Asaarh aaya ghata chhayi gagan par
Rasawat man mera rasiya sajan par

(The month of Asaarh has come, the clouds cover the sky
My heart pines for my feckless beloved)

In almost all the *barahmasas* studied in Alvi's collection, the poet emerges as a *sutradhar* (a narrator-cum-one-man-chorus). On a single strand of separation from the beloved, he strings together the same stock of images and metaphors: *sooni sej* (the lonely bed), *piya bin* (without the beloved), *koel ki kook* (the sound of the cuckoo), *rasiya sajan* (feckless beloved), etc. In several *barahmasas*, such as those by the poet Wahab written to resemble a Bhojpuri *lok geet*, the love for the *pir* is reflected in the anguished cry of the *virahini*. Here, the poet employs the traditional Sufi concepts of *ishq-e-haqiqi* (the love of the real world) and *ishq-e-majazi* (transcendent or metaphysical love). Here, one is reminded of Amir Khusro who, upon the death of his beloved *pir*, Hazrat Nizamuddin Aulia, had expressed his grief thus:

Gori sowe sej par much pe dare kes
Chal Khusro ghar aapne, rain bhayi pardes

(The beloved sleeps upon her couch, her face covered with her tresses
Come, Khusro, let us go home, for night falls in these strange lands)

The weft of mysticism thus intertwines with the warp of love in almost all the *barahmasas* right from the time of Afzal and his *Bikat Kahani*. Perhaps unsurprisingly, then, scholars such as Alvi have pointed to the influence of classical Persian mystic poets such as Jami and Rumi on Afzal. This is amply evident in verses such as the Persian one below which, roughly translated, means that the abode of the beloved is better than the mosque and the Kaaba:

Ba masjid kaaba-dayaar ishq ast
Ba daar-o kucha-o bazaar ishq ast

Agar bardar baasi humcho Mansur
Nabashi az dar-e- dildaar mehjur

In fact, the *barahmasa* had none of the ribald innuendo and sexual tension of the *rekhti* poetry which was often written either as a tribute to the courtesan (a woman considered to be beyond the pale of polite society) or centered around the tensions between women in an entirely sequestered and cloistered society, such as those between sisters-in-law or between mother-in-laws and daughters-in-law which found an outlet through suggestive if not outright risqué jokes and innuendoes. The element of the ribald and the risqué is entirely missing in the *barahmasa*; it contends itself solely and entirely with the *virahini* pining for her missing mate.

Also, redolent as it is with the language of Krishna *bhakti*, Braj-bhasha lent itself with natural ease to songs of yearning and longing for a beloved who was often away and was rumoured to be dallying with others. So we have examples of poets attempting verses in Braj that come close to the *barahmasa* right up till the late nineteenth and early twentieth centuries. Writing under the pen-name of 'Brijbhashi', the remarkable figure of Syed Muttalibi Faridabadi (1893-1978), who worked actively with the Kisan Sabhas in the Mathura area and later also with the progressive writers, wrote a drama called *Kisan Rut* and a collection of poems called *Haiya Haiya*; but by now the rigour of maintaining the 12-month sequence had leached out. Muttalibi Faridabadi adopted the novel device of making nature the *sutradhar* in his play, *Kisan Rut*; while this was an interesting innovation, this kind of writing was a far cry from the *barahmasa* of Afzal or Najeeb or Waheed.

Barahmasas began to be printed by the 1860s, the last one being written almost a hundred years ago. With Urdu becoming a cosmopolitan language, its roots to the soil gradually loosened; the pastoral and rural were relegated to the crude and unrefined that needed to be weeded out.

To reemphasize an interesting point: while the *barahmasas* concerned themselves with the women's world, adopted a woman's voice and spoke of a woman's needs, none were actually written by women poets. The *barahmasa*, then, emerges as a body of work almost entirely of the female voice (*zenani boli*), but written by a male composer and from a male perspective. This vocal masquerade of men speaking in women's voices ended as the narrator's voice became a male one; the feminine narrator and feminine sensibilities increasingly began to be associated with effeminacy whereas the ghazal—the model against which the *barahmasa* was counterpoised—became the vehicle for 'high' culturc.

The binaries of high and low also included the oral and textual, folk and classical, masculine and feminine, fixed and fluid. A study of the *barahmasas* thus shows not merely how word was lost to text, and orality to textuality, but also how pluralism was replaced by Unitarianism, multiculturalism by puritanism, the feminine-gendered narration by the masculine, and inclusion by exclusion.

Single Women, Self-love, and the Gender of Waiting

DEBOTRI DHAR

> *Wait for him. Nothing is lovelier than a woman waiting for her man to return home, or on a date, in spite of him being late. He might feel bad once he comes in, but he will surely love you so much more just for the fact that you waited for him to come back.*
>
> —11 Things that Mean More to Men than "I Love You"[133]

'Am I in love? Yes, since I am waiting. The other one never waits. Sometimes I want to play the part of the one who doesn't wait; I try to busy myself elsewhere, to arrive late; but I always lose at this game. Whatever I do, I find myself there, with nothing to do, punctual, even ahead of time. The lover's fatal identity is precisely this: I am the one who waits.' This is Roland Barthes in *A Lover's Discourse*,[134] tracing the dark-light shapes of loving and waiting as shadow-selves, mutually and inextricably bound. Barthes: philosopher, post-structuralist, semiotician, literary critic. In working through the complex layers of his—*his*—fragments on love, a pronoun can also become a 'writerly text' amenable to multiple interpretations. So, death of the author[135] or not, here is the reader—I, *she*—immersed in the impossibility of taking the man out of Barthes, and Barthes out of the man, to ask, by way of catharsis: what is the *gender* of love's waiting?

Also, might there be a link, howsoever tenuous, between that and the gender of the author? For women's literature has, across cultures, functioned as a creative response to the historical marginalization of female experience within life and literature. Swinging between belonging and alienation within the rarefied ramparts of the mainstream—'*male*stream'—literary canon, women penned their protest through fiction. In *A Literature of Their Own*, Elaine Showalter thus famously termed women's writing a subculture.[136] Of course a writer does not have to be a woman to authentically engage with women's silenced histories, nor do all women writers necessarily use 'gynocriticism,' a framework proposed by Showalter to read texts though the lens of female experience. And why should literature even be identified by the gender of the author, for, as Joyce Carol Oates admits, a serious artistic voice concerns style and is sexless; but Oates herself argues later, to have a sex-determined voice is better than to have no voice at all.[137] Would some such sex-determined voices move us away from traditional presentations in literature in order to *re*present (the gender of) love's waiting differently: who waits for whom, why, and for how long? And, speaking of gender, what about single women? Must love—and love's waiting—always be for the other? What, instead, of *self*-love, especially for those whose identities were traditionally dictated by gendered ideas of passivity, sacrifice, and denial of the self?

It began with two male readers' responses to my novel *The Courtesans of Karim Street*,[138] whose plot may be described as women-centered. (The cast of characters does include many men, not to mention two countries, some trees, a smattering of old and new cities, languages, homes and histories, pasts and presents, and several pairs of emerald eyes. But alas, in the hallways of literary criticism, there is no such thing as an old-and-new-city-centered novel, or a tree-centered novel, much less an eye-centered one.) In any case, the novel's two—or three, if we include the unnamed narrator—main female characters *leave*, albeit in different ways. Megan Adams, an American academic, leaves, well, American academia, to come to India on the trail of an anonymous letter and the promise of a red-gold tree; but since she travels over the university Christmas holidays and returns to America to resume teaching in the spring term—ah, the cruelties of academic contracts, but we digress—she is not the subject of our interrogation. Instead, for the purpose of this essay, we are interested in, first, the novel's female narrator who has an extramarital affair, thus temporarily 'leaving' her husband and marriage; and second, Naina, an ambivalent inheritor of the courtesan tradition of north India, who decides to be single again and to travel abroad on a performing arts fellowship, leaving her relationship with a rather nice male character who remains back in India to work on the ruins of old Delhi (and for whom I, as the author, had begun to develop romantic feelings as I wrote him into being, such a heart he had, and such a soul...)

The female narrator's extramarital 'affair' of one afternoon invoked anger and disbelief in a male reader with whom I was personally acquainted; how *could* the wife of an important and *good* man have an irresponsible, even if very brief, affair with just *anybody*, he opined—until I had to remind him of the literary, social and psychological context of the female narrator's actions, her lifelong guilt, and that the 'anybody' in question was perhaps a 'good man' too, even if not as rich or 'important' as the husband. It also had to be pointed out to the reader in question, whose life choices we had been aware of for many years—and this is what had made me especially indignant—that he expected a *fictional* married woman in a novel to adhere to the laudable principle of marital fidelity, even for that one 'errant' afternoon, that he himself had never found necessary to adhere to over the course of his lifespan, in his *real* life as a married man. Interestingly enough, what had excessively troubled this male reader did not trouble many women, readers as well as reviewers, who interpreted the novel's women to be 'intelligible female characters with relatable predicaments.'[139]

Similarly, the character Naina's decision to leave her relationship upset another male reader who otherwise loved the novel; how, he asked, could Naina end a sweet love-story just to pursue her career? 'Your ideology got in the way of their love,' he stated flatly, referring to my academic training in Women's Studies, if not feminist beliefs. I conceded that writing is as deeply political an act as is reading; what we write and how we read are squarely situated within inherited and inhabited political and historical frames. Through our reading and writing practices, we either conform to or contest these frames; more frequently, we do both. In that sense, no art can be entirely devoid of ideology, not even dreamy romantic fiction, I said. Besides, the novel's plot treats dance not just as a career or a profession—such bland,

bland words—but also as passion, and resistance, despite the vicissitudes of history and the pathological framing of the courtesan tradition during the colonial era through a battery of imperialist laws, institutions, and medicalized narratives.[140] 'But still,' he replied. Naina doesn't want to end the relationship so much as she wants to find her own identity, I argued. Being from the walled city, the social class difference between him and her makes her uncomfortable in his boozy, glamorous South Delhi world; she wants to be more than just a rich man's wife, and strikes out on her own despite her fears. That takes courage, I said. But still, my friend maintained.

Fluctuating between indignation and angst—was he right? Was he wrong? Was it just a matter of perspective?—the writer in me re-read certain portions of the book where the first character, the narrator, speaks of her troubled childhood, foster-homes, the brief joys of a whirlwind wedding—'a time of such wild happiness, hotels with pretty balconies, beachfront restaurants, dancing in tune with the turquoise, tumbling music of the waves, foam in our faces, knolls of sand and seashells at our feet' (p. 213). And then, neglect, hugging her own silences once again, feeling closer to an old city than to her husband—'Like me, this city is full of buried worlds; it speaks to me, it understands' (p. 10)—her yearning for a 'happy song' (p. 110), the complexity of her choices, her illnesses, her guilt.

Then, the passages where the second character, Naina, is afraid to leave, but not afraid enough to stay; and when her boyfriend asks her a hard question—'Do you really think it's going to be a cakewalk abroad? No discrimination, an equal world, where you fit right in?'—she responds with, 'I've never lived in an equal world. I've never fit in. Not with my own people. Not with yours... I want to see new places, dance. I have hope. If we don't have hope, what do we have?' (p. 204) 'And for that, you want to end our relationship!' he says, to which she answers, 'It doesn't have to be forever. Afterwards...' (p. 204). Tearful, she says it's her fault—'I'll never forgive myself for causing you, us, this pain'—and he responds with a Ghalib couplet: '*Kee mere qatl ke baad usne jafaa se tauba, hae uss zud-pashiimaan ka pashiimaan hona*' (p. 204). Can their relationship be resumed if they remain in love with each other, he asks; she says yes. He wants to know if they will remain friends in the meantime; she reaches for his hand, their meeting thus ending on a note of hope. 'Stillness fell upon them, as weighty as a promise. The two of them walked in silence, along the still, moonlit landscape, and through the drowsing trees' (p. 204).

Do these passages signal the death of love-in-fiction, wrought by heartless female characters? (Or even heartless female novelists—I, she—wielding the pen?) *Butstillbutstill* came the resounding answer, through the frozen stillness of winter nights, from across the seven seas, until I realized, with a shiver, where the problem lay: in the *gender* of who waits for love.

*

Even a cursory glance at world literatures, broadly defined to include mythologies, fables and fairy-tales, literary and popular fiction, poetry and drama, reveals that traditionally, it was the elite and/or middle class woman who waited for the man—for the father, husband and sons she loved—to return from work, or war, while tending lovingly to the home and hearth.

Penelope, the wife of Odysseus in Homer's epic poem *Odyssey*, waits twenty years for her husband's return while he fights the Trojan War, turning away other suitors and remaining faithful to him as she stitches and un-stitches a burial shroud. Scarlett O'Hara of *Gone with the Wind* is ultimately left loving, and waiting for, Rhett Butler, who had ironically once loved her more. 'Tomorrow is another day,' Scarlett tells herself, as she stands framed against the looming silhouette of Tara, with the background music rising to a crescendo in the film version. For the middle class female protagonists of Charlotte Perkins Gilman's 'The Yellow Wallpaper' and Usha Priyamvada's *Pachpan Khambe Lal Deewarein*, love's waiting is endlessly painful. Strolling into a more ancient world of moats and magic wands, one finds Snow Whites, Cinderellas, and princess Rapunzels all waiting for their princes to come a-riding and rescue them from glass caskets, evil stepmothers, towers and dungeons. One of the few exceptions among fairytales is, perhaps, *Beauty and the Beast*; here love holds more power than looks or wealth, and the man/beast waits for her rather than she for him. What are some other instances of male literary characters waiting for love when the women leave, and under what circumstances?

Speaking of *bhasha* literature, an early example that comes to mind is of Nikhil, from India's first Nobel Laureate Rabindranath Tagore's Bengali novel *Ghare-Baire.*[141] Set in the Swadeshi period of India's struggle for independence, *Ghare-Baire* weaves a story around Nikhil, his wife Bimala, and his Swadeshi leader friend Sandip. Nikhil loves his wife deeply, encourages her education, and coaxes her to leave the traditional confines of the women's quarters (*zenana*) to engage with the outside world. Interpreting her husband's non-involvement in the freedom struggle as a lack of virility, Bimala becomes attracted to Sandip and his invocation of her as a powerful but chained symbol of India's womanhood. Feminist scholarship has long argued that nationalist ideology sets up woman simultaneously as victim and goddess, with women being framed as carriers of national culture and signifiers of cultural difference. Critics such as Cynthia Leenerts and Ashis Nandy have therefore read *Ghare-Baire* as a national allegory,[142] with Bimala representing India caught between the opposing ideologies of humanitarian internationalism and aggressive nationalism.

Ghare-Baire mirrors Partha Chatterjee's provocative essay which argues that nationalist ideology divided the domain of culture into the spiritual and the material, home and the world, *ghar* and *bahir*, educating the new woman outwardly but preserving her Indian femininity from within.[143] Bimala leaves her love for Nikhil owing to Sandip's firebrand nationalism; but with her subsequent realization of her folly, *Ghare-Baire* resolves Bimala's question on the same lines as Chatterjee's argument. Hence I have earlier read *Ghare-Baire* through the metaphor of 'home,' whether understood as material dwellings, geographical spaces, socio-psychic identities or imagined communities, and functioning as potential sites of confirmation and contradiction that not just protect, but have historically been organized around a pattern of inclusions and exclusions to keep the other out.[144] However, now re-thinking the novel's climax, a new and fascinating angle on love, gender and waiting presents itself. Roving eyes and multiple mistresses were then an accepted norm for wealthy zamindars, but Nikhil is devoted to Bimala; when she 'leaves' him, he waits patiently for her to return. Hence Bimala becoming a widow on the level of the plot—during a social period marked by tremendous ill-treatment and ostracism of widows, and despite her heart's ultimate restoration 'home' to her husband—functions as a literary trope, a punishment for her transgression of gender norms governing love, and who is allowed to leave.

Of course, 'Indian' or *bhasha* literature is not a monolith any more than 'Eastern' or 'Western' or 'English' literature is. Instead, varied literary and linguistic expressions find their unique identity within a shifting field of meanings, of centers and peripheries, and the named and unnamed positions in-between.

Edna O'Brien's short story 'Inner Cowboy,' a more contemporary piece bearing witness to the rich literary traditions of Anglo-Irish literatures, offers yet another interesting instance of a man who waits for love. 'Flat, watery land. Big lakes, little lakes, turloughs that filled up in the rain, and rivers a reddish brown from the iron in the soil.'[145] (p. 103) This is the Irish countryside of cut turf, mist and flying dust that is home to the story's main character, Curly. Peaceful, talks-to-himself, works-hard-and-does-not-quit-even-when-kicked-and-called-a-retard-by-his-boss Curly, who prefers the dun-brown bogs to the black, gritty quarries. Curly, briefly a hero after having delivered a calf, suddenly finds himself on the wrong side of the law for helping a friend hide some money that belongs to the big men with shiny chrome cars and shinier wives. He goes missing in the bog, his body stiff and blue from being in freezing water for hours when it is finally discovered. Curly, who always wanted to do something really wild, and to have a girlfriend to love. Love here is blue—blue as water, as watery land, as big lakes of hope and little lakes of despair—inking its absence through his life, and death; an eternal wait for living, and for love.

Another interesting male character who waits for love is the Tiger, in the allegorical novel *The Tiger's Wife* by Belgrade-born Tea Obreht.[146] The author's family left Yugoslavia when the war broke out, and war forms a charred backdrop to this tale that imaginatively weaves myth, history, and politics. A tiger escapes from a zoo bombed by the Nazis and heads for the fictional mountain village of Galina, whose inhabitants include the brooding butcher-musician Luca, his deaf-mute Muslim wife, and a young boy. Luca, hounded by his own demons, inflicts unimaginable terrors on his wife, mangling her ribs, scalding her skin, bludgeoning, breaking her body and soul. Luca disappears one day; and when she begins to stroll smilingly around the village, bruiseless and frcc, and her belly begins to swell, the village is rife with gossip that 'The tiger is her husband. He comes into her house each night and takes off his skin' (p. 219). Even the famed hunter Darisa, there to kill the tiger, hallucinates that he stands 'in front of the house of the tiger's wife and watched the return of her husband, broad-shouldered, red skin glinting in the moonlight, cross the square and come down the road, the night behind him drawing in like the hem of a dress. The door of the butcher's house would open, and then, through the window, Darisa could see the tiger rise upright and embrace the girl...' (p. 260).

To the young boy who grows up to be the narrator's grandfather, however, 'the baby was incidental. He had no need to guess that it was a result of some drunken stupor of Luca's, or rape by some unnamed villager, and that the baby had been there before the tiger had come to

Galina' (p. 220). Instead, he longs for his Shere Khan, both real and imagined, and wonders why the villagers cannot understand that the cold, hungry tiger means no harm, that he sees 'the girl as she had seen him: without judgment, fear, foolishness, and somehow the two of them understood each other without exchanging a single sound' (p. 220). When the girl doesn't come, the tiger waits. He agonizes when he has to go 'a week without the warmth of the village and the smokehouse smell of her hair, though he had found faint traces of her in the air now and then, almost always at night' (p. 261). When the pain of separation could no longer be borne, 'Once or twice he had gone to her, had tracked her down in the blackness of the trees, but she had always led him back' (p. 261). Can this tender story of a woman and a tiger—interspecies love, as it were—have a conventionally happy ending? Of one thing we can be sure: male, but not human, and entirely unschooled in the gendered rituals of 'civilized' society, the tiger is able to love, to surrender, and to wait, with the fullness and humanity that perhaps only an animal sometimes can.

Several other literary works offer interesting perspectives on the complex relationship between love, gender, and waiting. Vikram Seth's novels *A Suitable Boy* (1993) and *An Equal Music* (1999) are an instance. *A Suitable Boy* is set in post-independence India, and weaves together a range of sub-plots including political and economic reforms, caste relations, and religious tension as the backdrop to a mother's search for a suitable groom for her daughter. *An Equal Music* is the story of a professional violinist who finds his lost love—a pianist who is now married, has a young son, and is slowly going deaf—and has an affair with her, only to lose her again. Both novels are ultimately love stories, their sensitive exploration of romance and relationships being not just one dimension of Seth's oeuvre but an overarching theme uniting disparate works that has been noted by several critics, making Seth one of the few male writers in contemporary Indian English literature who has received critical and popular acclaim for penning fiction in this under-theorized and largely misunderstood genre. What is interesting is that in Seth's literary world, men and women are broadly similar; men suffer political, social and personal loss alongside women, women are as capable of inflicting pain, and love's waiting is un-gendered.

It might be argued that this is how it is in life too, and that the pains inflicted in and by love have never been middle class heterosexual women's alone. Here we might reference 'intersectionality,' the idea that gender is by no means the only form of discrimination, given the ways in which gender intersects with the insistent inequalities of race, class, caste, nationality, religion, and sexual orientation, locally and globally, to create complex structures of power. But here too, many women writers have probed deeper into the larger structural conditions that weigh against particular women in particular ways, demonstrating that no matter how privileged a certain section of society may be, the women of that section are less so. Much like the forbidden love in Arundhati Roy's novel *The God of Small Things* (1997), the story of a traditional Syrian Christian family in Ayemenem, Kerala, whose divorced daughter Ammu falls in love with the 'low caste' Velutha. The discovery of Ammu's relationship coincides with the accidental death of Sophie, Ammu's Oxford-returned brother's daughter from his English ex-wife. Velutha is falsely implicated, arrested and brutally tortured by the police, and dies in custody. Ammu's children are taken away from her and from each other, and she commits suicide far away from home. Love and loss are inseparably intertwined here, a rebellious woman from a middle class 'respectable' family and a lower caste man saddled by centuries of caste oppression ultimately united in their powerlessness. Here, too, waiting is forever, with not just love but also justice being endlessly deferred.

*

Thus, a closer examination of the vast corpus of world literatures, broadly defined, reveals that if much of literature is about love, leaving and waiting, then our literary imaginations have historically been profoundly gendered. In many cases, a tenuous link also emerges between the gender of the author and their representation, stylization, voice. Thus fairy-tales written mostly by men deployed convenient categories and simplistic binaries: the princess, the damsel in distress, the evil stepmother, the witch. This would also be true of Homer's *Odysseus* and, with some qualifications, of many religious epics. Speaking of Bengali renaissance literature, penned at a time when the fight for women's emancipation was led by elite men (unlike in the United States, where first-wave feminism was led by elite women) such that male writers like Tagore wrote about women's issues, we still find subtle differences between their work which subordinated gender to 'larger' themes such as family, religion and critiques of aggressive nationalism, and that of women writers like Asha Purna Debi who foregrounded the women's movement. The same might be said for later writers discussed earlier, like Charlotte Perkins Gilman and Usha Priyamvada, and many others such as Anita Nair, whose novel *Mistress* I have elsewhere interpreted to be a postcolonial feminist reworking of the Radha-Krishna love story.[147] Therefore, while women writers have taken up a variety of literary themes and positions such that it is impossible to generalize, one might tentatively conclude that any link between gender and love also extends to the thematic and stylistic treatment of leaving and waiting.

In reflecting upon my own conscious and subconscious literary choices in this regard, I realized that I was, since childhood, filled with a desire to re-write—re-gender, as it were—mythology, fairy tales and folklore, both 'Indian' and 'Western'. I wanted to somehow undo my beloved Krishna's leaving Radha for the 'larger' pursuit of statecraft, and Ram's treatment of Sita, and always felt that Snow White should have married one of the dwarfs; who knows how the rich, handsome prince would turn out, but the dwarfs with their surpassing beauty and tender strengths would love her forever. The exquisite brutality of *The Little Mermaid* still sits inside me like a knife; that fish-tailed nymph, swimming out of the seas for the love of her prince, only to find herself in a bluer world where love's waiting never ends.

My first novel was published when I was a teenager, and while it drew upon some themes dear to my heart—women's independence, travel, cultural collisions, and love—the resolution of love's dilemma played out in conventional terms, with the woman waiting for the man. However, in my short story collection *Postcards from Oxford: Stories of Women and Travel*, women travelers had begun to cross not just geographical but also social, economic, emotional and psychic boundaries of all kinds. As a review in the *New York Journal of Books* noted: 'The trajectory of the road was once considered a strictly masculine pursuit. A lady's place was in the parlor, or perhaps the boudoir. Yes, female walkers certainly existed, including George Sand, Rene Vivien and Djuna Barnes to name but a few; however, the urban adventurer was predominantly male. The women we encounter in Ms. Dhar's work seize the trajectory of the road and navigate it on their own terms. As a body of work, they examine what it means for a 21st century woman to travel.'[148] *The Courtesans of Karim Street* carried forward this theme of women's travel, and of female friendships across divides; yet, the two male readers' reactions that sparked this essay point to the dogged persistence of gender asymmetries. Or else, given our cultural appreciation of men who focus on issues 'larger' than love (even as one or more women wait for them to return), why would a literary sub-plot featuring a man who waits for the love of a woman while she travels overseas for work and also supports her family, invite angst or condemnation?

The irony here is also that modern India is filled with real instances of women travelling alone for education and work, especially among the urban middle classes, such that the phenomenon is not unknown at all. Indeed, it would be incorrect to identify this social phenomenon as restricted *only* to the urban middle classes, their economic or other privileges notwithstanding; if anything, the sheer numbers of women from rural areas and small towns who travel to urban and cosmopolitan centers in India for education and work is as impressive. Nor would it be impossible to find single women from earlier periods of history who defied their own social circumstances to travel alone such that the differences within and across time periods, then, pertain largely to context and scale. And to the extent that women have travelled, there must have been men who waited—for them, for love, for marriage. But still?

It may, in fact, be validly argued that in 2020, why do the goalposts for women compulsorily need to be marriage and motherhood? Not all single women are 'waiting', or being waited for, by possible partners. Many women are not just getting married later and later in life, but also choosing not to get married at all. More importantly, remaining single in today's times does not necessarily mean that one is celibate, 'on the shelf,' or spinsters in a traditional sense who were once framed as bitter or unhappy figures worthy only of pity and social condescension. Instead, some women, especially from more privileged sections of society, see singlehood as a choice that may allow greater professional and creative focus, a way to explore and establish one's own identity in the world.

It goes without saying that the choice to remain single holds intriguing implications for women writers and the characters they pen. In *A Room of One's Own* (1929), Virginia Woolf had spoken passionately of the material, educational, and social limitations faced by women to argue that a woman must have money and 'a room of her own' if she is to write. Since such money for women was, at the time, a consequence primarily of birth and marriage—i.e. a rich father and/or socially highly positioned husband—the traditional route for women writers was (and, in some settings, still continues to be) one that continued to uphold marriage as the norm for women. For all the social acceptance and economic support that such a traditional route historically provided for middle class women, singlehood has allowed women artists, especially those who are positioned to avail of the opportunities afforded by education and social milieu, the space to focus more on their craft. As bell hooks writes in 'Women Artists:

The Creative Process' about 'what it means to have the luxury of time—time spent collecting one's thoughts, time to work undisturbed. This time is space for contemplation and reverie. It enhances our capacity to create…it is this stillness, this quietude, needed for the continued nurturance of any devotion to artistic practice—to one's work—that remains a space that women (irrespective of race, class, nationality etc.) struggle to find…We have yet to create a culture so transformed by feminist practice that it would be common sense that the nurturance of brilliance for the creation of a body of work fundamentally requires such undisturbed hours. In such a world it would make perfect sense for women who devote themselves to artistic practice to rightfully claim that space.'[149]

For those whose identities were historically constructed around gendered ideas of (often one-sided) sacrifice and denial of the self, learning to love one's self and cultivating one's own talents can be liberating. Yet for all the changes in society, ancient patterns do find ways to reassert themselves. A case in point is the Airtel advertisement where a professionally qualified modern Indian couple are not just each other's office colleagues, but the wife is the husband's boss; while the 'boss' asks her subordinate to work overtime and complete the project, the wife in her rushes back home to prepare dinner. While an outrage on Twitter followed, many defended the ad with 'what is wrong with a wife cooking dinner for an overworked husband,' 'perhaps she likes to cook,' 'Indian women are different from Western women,' etc. While even I like to cook—the culinary is an art form, I would argue—it does seem that the third defense is problematic because of its cultural essentialism, the sharp binary it draws between cultures without taking into account that 'Indian women' do not constitute a monolith whose values, lifestyles, and personal and professional interests and responsibilities are all the same. In any case, whatever may be our own personal and political stand, it cannot be denied that when the 'boss-wife' calls to tell him that she is waiting for him, the advertisement restores the so-called 'natural' (but in reality, social) order of not just whose duty it is to be in the kitchen (at a time when more dual income couples are moving towards a sharing of household chores), but also, in the context of this essay, whose gendered duty it is to *wait* for love.

As one continues to ponder over women's choices in life and literature, I am reminded of a newspaper column I wrote a few years ago, while teaching at a liberal arts college. Apart from describing the winding roads of Wooster, in Ohio, the column referenced inter continental travel, the adventures of being associated with universities worldwide, and being single; the piece enjoyed much online popularity, and many readers even in the United States assumed I was male. Afterwards, someone reasoned that this was because my name and its gender was culturally and linguistically unfamiliar, but my counter reasoning was this: with the name remaining the same, had the piece been about giving up a career, raising a child, cooking for the family, and waiting, lovingly, for a spouse to return home from work, war, or travel, would the audience still have assumed my gender to be male? Yes, love's (in)decisions, love's choices, even love's waiting...there have been very few words as profoundly gendered as the word 'love.'

Same-sex Love in India

PARVATI SHARMA

As I write this, the decades-old legal battle against Section 377 of the Indian Penal Code, its 'anti-gay' law, has taken its final turn. On 6 September 2018, five judges of the Indian Supreme Court delivered four separate but concurring judgements to declare, over almost five hundred pages, that consensual intercourse between adults cannot, indeed should not, be proscribed.[150]

Some months earlier, in July, these five judges had spent a week listening to arguments for and against the 158-year-old law that does precisely that. By many accounts, the bench was sympathetic towards its LGBT petitioners. The *Times of India* reported how Menaka Guruswamy and Jayna Kothari, two of the lawyers arguing against Section 377, 'lit up the courtroom with their arguments' and how one of the judges 'curtly brushed aside the objection' of an opposing counsel.[151] On Twitter, an observer described a day's hearing as 'empathetic and invigorating'.[152] There was every reason to hope that Section 377 would never again be debated in the country's courts.

It was a hope that began gathering pace the previous

year. On 24 August 2017, a nine-judge bench of the Supreme Court delivered a widely acclaimed judgement declaring privacy a 'fundamental right', which was seen to have wide-ranging implications, not least for the 'legality' of homosexuality. On the issue of privacy and sexual orientation, the judgement disapproved of an earlier Supreme Court verdict (*Suresh Kumar Koushal vs. Naz Foundation*) that held, in 2013, that the court would not 'read down'[153] the controversial law because, amongst other things, it applied only to a 'minuscule minority' and was hardly ever used. The Privacy judgement, however, asserted that the 'right to privacy and the protection of sexual orientation lie at the core of the fundamental rights guaranteed by Articles 14, 15 and 21[154] of the Constitution'. It went on to argue that even if Section 377 is rarely used, its very existence is 'constitutionally impermissible' because it creates a 'chilling effect' on individuals, one that arises from 'the danger of a human being subjected to social opprobrium or disapproval, as reflected in the punishment of crime'. Thus, it concluded,

> The *Koushal* rationale that prosecution of a few is not an index of violation is flawed and cannot be accepted. Consequently, we disagree with the manner in which *Koushal* has dealt with the privacy-dignity based claims of LGBT persons on this aspect.

Such unambiguous disagreement came at an apposite time: not only was a review of the 2013 *Koushal* judgement pending, another petition challenging the very constitutionality of Section 377 had also been introduced before the Supreme Court in 2016. Barely five months after its judgement on privacy, the Court referred that 2016 petition to a Constitutional Bench: the five empathetic judges who have, now, undone the *Koushal* ruling. In so doing, they have upheld an even older judgement, from 2009, when the Delhi High Court 'decriminalized' homosexuality—or, at least, certain sexual acts and homosexuality by implication—by changing a law too coy to criminalize homosexuality *except* by implication.

Over the years, this law, Section 377, has become as familiar to me as a song that's always on the radio. 'Whoever voluntarily has carnal intercourse against the order of nature with any man, woman or animal,' it intones, 'shall be punished with imprisonment for life, or with imprisonment of either description for term which may extend to ten years, and shall also be liable to fine.' The 'explanation' that follows doesn't really make things clearer: 'Penetration is sufficient to constitute the carnal intercourse necessary to the offense described in this section'. It is precisely the point, of course, that the offense is *not* described, and thus moved from the realm of the merely criminal to that of the unsayable. Thomas Babington Macaulay, who framed the Indian Penal Code, was clear he didn't want to 'give rise to public discussion on this revolting subject' and was therefore willing to lose in clarity of law what he would gain in purity of social morals. In other words, like people across ages and cultures, Macaulay just didn't want to talk about it.

Twenty years ago, when I was in college and falling madly in love with a girl, neither did I. This was about the time that Deepa Mehta's *Fire*, featuring a 'lesbian' romance that was as trite as it was controversial, released in India. Theatres were vandalised; counter-protests were held. One of these featured a woman with short hair holding a placard that proclaimed her 'Indian and Lesbian'. On me, that photograph had a literally chilling effect: it gave me goose bumps. No threat or inducement on this planet could have made me join that woman or admit, even to myself, that I had anything in common with her.

In those pre-Internet days, I thought myself entirely alone, both in my fear and my infatuation. In not wanting to have anything to do with lesbians, however, I was very much part of a crowd. A fairly representative article from the time complained that 'the broader issue of freedom of expression and tolerance had got derailed' by 'placard-waving lesbians'; and quoted a 'surprised' Deepa Mehta herself as saying, 'I can't have my film hijacked by any one organisation. It is not about lesbianism. It's about loneliness, about choices.'[155]

I chose to continue writing lovelorn letters to the girl I was in love with, stay far away from community organising, and quickly grow my hair. This was not my best idea; the girl stopped talking to me, I had no Indian lesbians to turn to, and my tangled hair fell out when I tried to comb it. With all the clear thinking of my twenty-one years, I decided to date a boy.

This was a disaster in many ways, but for the purposes of this essay one particularly disastrous night will do: one evening, he told me that one of his friends had said I might be lesbian. I couldn't believe it—what about all my knotted hair? The chills returned. I lived on a university campus then, and I got on the first bus out of it. I went all the way to my house, across the city, and sat a long while at the bus stop... because what was the point? How could I face my mother with 'lesbian' written all over my face, as it obviously was?

So, I walked. It wasn't very late, but a winter darkness had fallen. I walked under bridges and past roadside markets. I stopped at a phone booth to make a blank call to that girl, whom I still loved. I walked along busy main roads, hopping off and on pavements, my hands deep in the pockets of my baggy sweatshirt, my head in its hood. I walked, alternately worried that everyone could tell I was depraved, and relieved that nobody could tell I was a girl. Finally, I took the last bus back to the university. When I got off near my hostel, I saw the boy I was dating waiting outside it. I turned and walked to a deserted school building nearby and spent the night on its porch, slapping ineffectively at mosquitoes.

Like Deepa Mehta, I too could say that this has nothing to do with lesbianism, that it is just my little story of loneliness and choices. And in this, too, I wouldn't be alone. Even lesbians—particularly lesbians—don't like to use the word. As Ashwini Sukthankar,[156] editor of *Facing the Mirror: Lesbian Writing from India*, points out in her introduction:

> [Lesbian] is such a difficult word, and unsettles even those of us who live out our love for women every day. We find it hard to claim the identity which accompanies that love, and we are intimidated by the social outrage it will bring. We trip over its syllables, stammer, find the sound sticking in the throat and try to work around it with gentler but specific alternatives, like 'gay', 'not straight', 'woman-loving' or 'dyke'.

It is a surprisingly difficult word, 'lesbian', for all that it flows so easily: the lingual 'l' preceding a soft sibilance, making way for the bilabial meeting of lips in a 'b'. Exuding sexuality in a way that the hard, monosyllabic edges of 'dyke', 'queer', 'gay' simply cannot, 'lesbian' marks those who are defined by it as women who *make* love to women, who actively seek out and create their own sexual pleasure. In societies that have traditionally valued duty and sacrifice over individual fulfilment, such brazen pandering to one's own self is not what 'nice girls'—and boys—are raised to do. One way, then, to make the word and idea acceptable is to drape it in despair. As Poorva Rajaram remarked on a mailing group, she's tired of newspapers calling her with the assumption that 'being lesbian... in India is the degree zero of all pathos'.

So, while a great deal of breath is often wasted on whether homosexuality is a choice or not, the broader social disapproval of homosexuality stems from a choice that homosexuals *do* make: whether to live and love as we desire, or to pretend otherwise. As Nithin Manayath writes of his first visit to a support group in Bangalore and its more compelling aftermath:

> The meeting went on, minutes were taken. What was more important for me came afterwards, when we all trotted to a couple's home. To me, and to others in the group, their existence, as a couple who kept house together and went on to do so for eight years, was important.[157]

When you realise you're not 'normal', to live normally is always the first and most hopeless ambition; and yet, paradoxically, this choice—to extend your homosexuality beyond furtive groping to open squabbles about the milk—is often interpreted as choosing to cast your naked sexuality over the humdrum decorum of the dining table, as choosing selfish pleasure over social duty—and makes homosexuality both incomprehensible and reprehensible to so many.

Vivek Shanbhag, author of the chilling family drama *Ghachar Ghochar*, notes in an interview that, 'unlike in the West, the smallest unit of society in India is a family, not an individual'.[158] As Sandip Roy discovers when he returns to live in India as a gay man after twenty years abroad, it's his lack of family, not love of men, that makes a real mystery of him: 'I had not reckoned that what would be truly difficult was being an unmarried man, especially an unmarried man living part of the time on his own, away from family. That was what was regarded as profoundly abnormal'.[159] In their introduction to *Same-Sex Love in India: Readings from Literature and History*, Ruth Vanita and Salim Kidwai trace the logic of such social prioritising to its conclusion:

> The family is also the only form of social security and old-age insurance available to most people. This means that heterosexual marriage and parenthood hold many attractions even for homosexually inclined people. Many deal with the dilemma by marrying and then leading a double life. But the double life that was more socially viable in earlier periods now has to be more hidden since the domestic space has become more fiercely contested.[160]

Arguably, however, this contest hasn't been sparked by 'deviant' sexuality alone (or even as such) but rather by the elevation of romantic monogamy above all other kinds of love,[161] and thus the rise of 'selfish' sexuality regardless of its orientation.

Only a few days before the Privacy judgement, the *Indian Express* carried this headline on its front page: 'Live-ins are type of social terrorism: Rights panel chief'. For all the shock-and-awe of the headline, Justice Prakash Tatia, chairperson of the Rajasthan human rights commission, was making a rather plaintive argument:

> According to him, live-in relationships have a detrimental effect on the institutions of family, and that children born

> of such relationships are not accepted by society. 'What is the effect on family... on one's daughter of a marriageable age? On the son? If we ignore all this, we are individuals... we have no right to say we live in society or with dignity because we are not relevant for others and others are not relevant for us... they (couples living-in) live outside society,' he said.[162]

A similar bewilderment runs through this report from 2014: 'Homosexuality is unnatural, leading psychiatrist says'. In fact, the headline is as leading as the psychiatrist, a former president of the Indian Psychiatric Society, who tells the newspaper that, 'The manner in which homosexuals have brought *the talk of sex* to the roads makes people uncomfortable. It's unnatural. Our society doesn't talk about sex. Heterosexuals don't talk about sex. It's a private matter' (emphasis mine).[163]

There are various ways to think about these grumblings. On the one hand, the Justice and the Doctor can be said to represent all that is wrong with Modern Indian Society, the conservative group-think that spreads its tentacles into every aspect of our lives, from rote-learning to sycophancy. 'Why won't you do what you should?' is what they're really saying, and one answer, of course, is that poetry and light bulbs don't come from doing what one 'should'; that doing what one 'should' promotes fear of authority (not least the authority of the mob), which no sane society could possibly want. Less dramatically, though, doing what one 'should' can also be seen as infantilising a people. Sumati Murthy and Sunil Mohan, activists with LesBIT, are often called to rescue runaway lesbian couples from the police. In such situations, they say, they are constantly having to remind the police that 'these people are adults'.[164]

In an essay that extends the arguments around 'decriminalising' homosexuality to arguments around legalising BDSM—more complicated terrain as it involves the right of a person to surrender to physical harm—Namita Avriti Malhotra and Nitya Vasudevan reach this compelling conclusion:

> Looking at S/M helps us to see how the state's desire itself is implicated... in the erotic fantasy of controlling the citizen and their sexual subjectivities and policing their fantasies and practices. However, the prohibitions of the state are hardly being played out on the passive, docile body of the citizen. What are these fantasies and desires that are being suggested here? Are they fantasies of errant citizens that can be disciplined and reformed?... Or are they fantasies of an infantile public, asking to be rescued from the 'morbid stage of sleaze' or 'malevolent modernity' that it may fall into?[165]

Only get married (to the right person), have children (at the right time) and remember to put away twenty per cent of your income into long term savings—and then, if you must love your partner, or if you must, instead, love your sister-in-law, if you must, indeed, love at all, well, of course you may do so, discreetly and in your spare time. As one lesbian titles her poignant evocation of a life lived in constant deferment of 'selfish' pleasure: 'Always in Due Course'.[166]

Of course, deferment may also elide into duplicity, and thus the indubitable frissons of *secret* pleasures; hidden passions are not necessarily unexpressed. Another self-confessed secret lesbian, Abha, quoted by Naisargi N. Dave in *Queer Activism in India: A Story in the Anthropology of Ethics*, mourns the 'beauty of silence' that once shrouded lesbian relationships:

> 'Secrecy, contrary to what you people think, is not a bad thing. There is tremendous spiritual possibility in those bonds. The LGBT gain has been a loss in these ways.'

One could read this as an internalisation of one's own prison, of people's sadly elastic ability to get used to just about any kind of injustice and privation. Or, one could read this more gently, even optimistically, as Dave does: for Abha, 'lesbian politics has turned a beautiful act of imagination into a disenchanted bore'.[167]

Having tried to 'un-gay' myself by running away, dating boys and growing my hair, I finally took an about-turn. I cut my hair. I came home and faced the mirror, quite literally, and I recognized myself. Over the next fifteen years, I came out, to friends, to family, and eventually in my writing. For anyone who cares to know, now, I am lesbian, and I cannot say I miss pretending I'm not... and yet.

For a decade I have been in a relationship, a committed and fulfilling love, and one that my partner and I have not tried, nor wanted, to hide from anyone—except that we (probably) won't ever define ourselves to *every* single member of our families, or larger circle of acquaintances. To put it another way: we are unlikely to declare ourselves wife and wife.

Does this silence bother me? My mother likes to say, 'For a writer, you can be really inarticulate!' Sometimes my partner and I fight, and I say, 'I don't want to be pretending!' But *am* I pretending? I'm no longer sure. Does it really bother me, inhabiting this grey area between being accepted and being accepted exactly on my terms? The more I think about it, the more I can only resort to a teenage mumble: I don't know. Maybe. Sometimes, sure, but not always.

And would we be *entirely* different if we were not

Indian, or living in India? The engagingly clever Australian comedy *Please Like Me* stars a twenty-something Josh, who stumbles upon his gayness in the first episode, and reacts to the idea of coming out with ennui rather than the traditional trepidation. When his boyfriend insists that he wants to meet Josh's parents (*as* his boyfriend) Josh whines he doesn't *want* to—'coming out is so 90s!' Is this what the much-decried decadence of the West has come to? Is coming out uncool, unless, maybe, you find a way to do it ironically? Or should I exclaim, like the Dad in that recurring *Goodness Gracious Me* skit: 'Indian!' We thought of it first.

And have I, after all, misjudged the worth of declaring the truth, the whole truth, at all times? In coming out, I did not do what I should, and it was exhilarating as often as it was terrifying, but it certainly did not give me a sudden freedom or ability to do (exactly and always) what I want. In that sense, the end that my partner and I have arrived at is similar in many ways: she *does* do what she should, and does it wonderfully well, and yet maintains the space in which to do what she wants. The more I've seen her engage with the dilemmas I've faced, in very different ways, the more I've realised that doing what one should, in its best form, is not necessarily unthinking, soul-stultifying or infantilising at all. It's very adult behaviour, in fact, to be responsible, to care for the good of the many as well as for the happiness of one's own self. Responsibility confers great agency upon a person, and to be responsible for those you love means ensuring their dignity together with your own. If it is essential for my dignity that I declare myself gay, perhaps it is essential for my family's dignity to never quite speak of it directly. From this perspective, 'coming out' is not so much a revelation of identity, but, in consonance with its continuous tense, a kind of slow, unfolding dance in which both sides learn the steps as they go along; a dance that, if done honestly and well, requires an expansion of spirit and heart on both sides, not just declarations and ratifications of identity.

The question of how much to reveal, to whom and how, is a recurring motif in gay lives; and it is mirrored, in a way, in the debate around Section 377. Amongst those who don't think homosexuality is a revolting disease, the debate is divided broadly into two strands: one argues that a change in law can propel a change in society, and the other that without broad social acceptance and support, a revised law can make little, if any, difference. In other words, would you rather have cut-and-dried legitimacy or negotiated acceptance; is there more to be gained from the legal right to call your partner your wife, or can we achieve more lasting change by nudging the limits of whatever social contract it is that allows us, now, to live out our days in implicit coupledom? 'Love at First Right' exclaimed *The Indian Express's* banner headline to celebrate the 377 ruling. A few days later, writing a personal essay for that newspaper on the subject, I felt all the trepidation I feel each time I reveal myself. Is it the law, alone, that determines a person's 'guilt'?[168]

Privacy is one of the flashpoints of this debate. On the one hand, the right to privacy is used to argue that people must have the right to do what they will with their bodies; on the other, it is said that privileging private rights may be ineffective, even detrimental, when it comes to the rights, for example, of hijras and men who do not have access to bedrooms, and of course women—for whom the private home may often be a site of tyranny. It is worth noting that only days after the Privacy judgment, the Indian government appeared before the Delhi High Court arguing that marital rape must not be criminalised because this would 'destabilise the institution of marriage', thus privileging the privacy of a 'marriage' over a woman's autonomy within it.

In India, the distinction between private and public is further complicated by the argument that here, homosexuality has been proscribed only legally (that too by a 'foreign' law) but socially 'tolerated'.[169]

Tolerance, however, lies in the eyes of the beholder. Take, for example, a scene from Valmiki's *Ramayana* that has Hanuman stumble upon a scene of homoerotic love between Ravana's wives. For Vanita and Kidwai, this demonstrates both the existence of, and lack of explicit injunction against, homosexuality in India's ancient past:

> Their being Rakshasa women may allow the author a certain freedom in his depiction of their sexual behaviour, but not all Rakshasas are represented by Valmiki as evil, and Hanuman also feels guilty about having violated the privacy of these women. He concludes that since his voyeurism happened inadvertently, it is pardonable.[170]

On the other hand, Mina Kumar, in 'Lesbians in Indian Texts and Contexts', argues that this scene

> [I]s set between descriptions of the beauty Hanuman first sees in Lanka and his dawning realisation that Lanka is evil. Thus lesbian relations are textually postulated as the gateway into degeneracy, a meeting place of good (beautiful women) and bad (lesbianism).[171]

Vanita and Kidwai also analyse how ancient and medieval Indian texts often 'fix' romantic non-conformity (whether hetero- or homosexual) via magic, prayer or re-birth. They explain the idea with two stories of a prince and a princess who fall in love with people of lower castes: in both cases, some form of divinity arrives to reveal that, in fact, the lower caste beloved held enviably high caste status in a previous birth. While it is possible, and possibly even encouraging, to extrapolate from this that pre-colonial India allowed for a certain fluidity between 'categories and boundaries'—it is a moot point whether being 'fixed' by metaphysical revisionism really dignifies or even legitimizes illicit (same-sex or inter-caste) attraction.

In any case, the 'choice' between legal legitimacy and social acceptability as it plays out in our lives is not really a choice, is it? I suspect most gay people, myself certainly, choose between self-assertion and self-effacement as instinctively as drivers 'choose' gears. You live and you love as a human being, not a category,[172] and while nobody's love is particularly original, everybody's love is unique; our chinks, our kinks, our fumblings are as particular to us as our dreams. Like dreams, too, love is intensely private—when you first fall in love, you don't want to talk about it to the world (though you may well not want to talk about anything else); and you certainly don't care what people will think or what judges will decide.

This is not, however, the privacy of bedrooms (or, not *only* the privacy of bedrooms) but the privacy of ecstasy. And when you love without the trappings that turn private ecstasy into social routine—marriage, family, children—when you insist on 'living-in' or being flagrantly lesbian, when you harbour the kind of love that depends upon itself to survive, you do, of course, unsettle the world; and that is no bad thing at all.

How to Write a Love Letter to a Tree

SUMANA ROY

Having grown up and fallen in love in a time before the immanent presence of the Internet, it was the reliable love letter that would preface most romantic encounters. It seemed so natural, such a given, that I didn't realise that a love letter was an object of utter privilege, not until Ranjit, our teenage house help, requested me to write a letter for him to give to Bobby, a voluptuous girl in our neighbourhood. He was, of course, illiterate—my mother had, with great diligence, taught him to sign his name. But no curriculum—or even homeschooling apparatus—trains one to write a love letter.

When I first went to boarding school as a sixteen-year old, I discovered this new world, away from the surveillance of censorious parents. It soon became my favourite genre of reading—I was amazed at the variety of ways in which love could be offered. This was a girls' boarding school, and so these letters came from that dirty word, and world, outside our 'pure' sanctuary: boys. We laughed at their silliness, at how awkwardly passion translated into words, their adoption of literary poses and postures, the spelling errors, their ambitions in love, as also, in spite of all of these, their closet shyness. Most of these letters did not get replies. We felt sad—most often a collective sadness—for them: that was all that our lubricated teenage egos would allow us to feel.

That loving is possible without words—without letter and letters—seems like an utter impossibility in a world of lovers with phones at their ears or their fingers on them, speaking and typing furiously. Watching them,as also oneself, in moments of self-consciousness, it becomes difficult to imagine love that can survive without the crutch of words. Only one-sided love, as between a decadently expensive handbag and a woman, doesn't need words.

I am a lover—this is one of my primary identities, and in an alternate world, I'd have put this as the first entry on my CV. Unfortunately, that doesn't seem to count for much, not in the professional world where love is pretty useless, and increasingly not in relationships either, where things besides love decide the fate of romantic relationships. And as I found, it also doesn't count if the object of one's affection is a non-human.

When I first became conscious of moving away from the social world, the first things I felt the need to abandon were the human rituals associated with love and courtship. To the non-human, these rituals would be a great source of entertainment. I allowed myself some self-critical laughter. There were a few other things I needed to rid myself of, such as the peculiar human obsession with monogamy and its definition of adultery. The world I was entering—the amoral world of plants—had no space for either of these artificial concepts, after all. A monogamous tree is not only an oxymoron but also a full-throated joke.

Perhaps because being a lover is my central, and default, identity, I found myself rejecting the botanist or environmentalist's investigative curiosity about plants. I wanted to know how one showed love to plants. It is amazing that there really is no way—no methodology, no ritual—of demonstrating one's love to a favourite, a beloved, tree. The rituals of human courtship are comic and tenuous, but long years of conditioning generate expectations. The things I had to abandon right at the outset were shyness and the semi-formal vanity associated with the rituals of courtship. There was also something else—I realised that I was in love not with one tree but with several, perhaps in love with all the trees there were. Do you realise what that made me in terms of a human equivalent? A woman in love with all the men in the world, an impossible female Don Juan?

Human lovers were terribly demanding. Trees did not seem to mind any lapses. Even if they did, there was no show of dissent or disapproval—that, as lovers would know, always brings more love. So, it was this first then, the abandoning and consequent adoption of grammars and syntaxes. The preface to any romantic relationship was, inevitably, a declaration of love. How did one declare it to a tree? I thought of the wounding scribbles on tree barks left by insecure human lovers—this display of literacy and confidence was, by some magic formula, meant to fuel or generate more, or perhaps permanent, love. But tattooing my name on the bark of a tree I loved seemed such a weird tautology. What was I to write? 'Mango + Sumana'? Wouldn't the human equivalent of that be 'Man + Sumana' tattooed on the forearm of a male lover? But all that was for later.

The relationship, and I was stubborn about calling it that, would need to be inaugurated at first, and it must come, my old human conditioning reminded me, with some ceremony. The love letter—mocked and desired at different times in my relationship with the world of men—was the first prop I found myself turning to. I could easily write a letter to a tree—so many before me had written odes—but there was the slight problem about comprehension. Lovers were, in any case, incomprehensible to each other; but this would involve more than the difficulties of translation. It would imply the invention of a new language, an alphabet, a font and grammar.

Had anyone tried this before me?

It turned out that someone indeed had. Katie Holten, an Irish artist, had, in her book *About Trees*, created an equivalent of a tree alphabet by a 'recycling' of texts.[173] The 256-page book contains tree-themed works by prominent authors and other luminaries, from Plato to Radiohead, via Jules Verne, Charles Darwin, and Zadie Smith that, considered together, provoke much thought about the relationship between humans and nature.

It was, of course, beautiful as an idea, that all that the best minds—I was allowing myself to ignore the familiar biases of the Western canon at the cost of the exclusion of other thought systems—had thought about trees had been condensed into a new vocabulary and that, in spite of the 'A for…' equivalence that seemed to drive identificatory mechanisms in learning, this might perhaps be one of the ways to articulate human love, romantic love, for trees. 'A for Apple, B for Beech, C for Cedar…' is clumsy, no doubt, but the fact that it was not the sound but a new visual mimetic alphabet—the representation of trees through the shapes of their trunks and branches—made it seem slightly closer to the comprehensibility of trees. The fact that trees do not have eyes, that reading, literacy, is not part of their life mechanism, didn't seem to matter, not to people who've wanted to write such love letters to trees, certainly not to me. That it was merely the substitution of one sense with another, sound with sight, did not seem to matter much either. I eventually wrote the three-word sentence—I love you—using Holten's tree alphabet, a tree for each letter.[174]

The choice of beautiful handmade paper on which to make this declaration suddenly seemed terribly embarrassing. Paper, made from trees, as the medium on which to courier my thoughts? The human equivalent of this would be using human hide to write a love note to a lover. Every step of this process made me realise the silliness, and often the outrageousness, of the romantic rituals involved in making the heart come out as it were, and reveal its secrets.

The love letter was evidence that love, to have a successful career, needed to abandon concealment, to give up its secretive life. For reciprocity, the foundation of romantic love, was possible only with the declaration of such love, its coming out of hiding. But for trees without a history of emotion, reciprocity was an alien notion. What this wish—to write a love letter to a tree—did to me was to unravel, one by one, with great subtlety, the silliness behind the premise of the love letter. And, in turn, to expose how unnecessary it was to 'real love', another grand arch of romantic love.

But I was a lover, a hopeless romantic, and I valued, against all empirical odds, self-expression in love. For non-artists like me, love was the closest approximation of the aesthetic experience. My life and its choices had been, and are, driven by love, and this, I thought, was the only way I could get to be an artist: by loving. Love was art. The rituals that had once come naturally, biologically, to humans and had now solidified into codes that survived on repetition, seemed tragicomic and unnatural when one imagined them playing out in the plant world. Wooing and courtship, letters and purposeful silences, rejection and promises of loyalty—all of these seemed such a farce when I thought of expressing them to a favourite tree. Also, I did not have one favourite tree; there were many. And somehow it did not seem immoral when that singular-plural distinction that decided character certificates in the social world were transferred into the plant world. The love letter seemed slightly polyamorous too—again I was reminded of a human social equivalent, and how it seemed like using hand-me-down letters from former lovers to a new one.

This frustration with the human discourse—both the manner of demonstrating love and the medium adopted to express it—drove me to the man who I thought had come closest to understanding them: Jagadish Chandra Bose, the botanist, physicist, writer and wearer of several other hats. It is a textbook aphorism now that Jagadish Bose was the first to 'discover' that plants were 'sentient beings'. Bose, like me, had been desperate for reciprocity, to turn this one-sided love into a dialogue, and he had therefore, propelled by this desire, turned to science, to devise instruments—spyware, as it were—to get trees and plants to communicate, or to use my metaphor, write or reply to my love letters.

There was the Resonant Recorder that could calibrate the level of excitement generated by external stimulus; the electric probe could identify parts of the plant which behaved like neurons in humans; the Phytograph recorded the heartbeat-like rhythms of the Desmodium plant; the famous Crescograph, for which Bose was praised and ridiculed in equal measure, recorded a plant's rate of growth in its own 'script' as it were. 'The secret of plant life was thus for the first time revealed by the autographs of the plant itself. This evidence of the plant's own script removed the longstanding error which divided the vegetable world into sensitive and insensitive,' Bose declared to the world in a lecture in the winter of 1917.[175]

In the famous essay titled 'Automatism in Plant and Animal', published in the *Modern Review* in 1908,[176] Bose begins by talking about the response of plants to light, to poison, to heat and cold, and in all these cases, he draws comparisons with the human body, most often with the human heart. Then he begins describing the behaviour of Desmodium, the telegraph plant, 'whose pulsation goes on perpetually, like the human heart'.[177] Bose records the 'nervous' behaviour of plants and posits them against the human. Like a lover, he wants some sign of communication that will tell him that they are aware of his existence, of his affection; he looks for 'spontaneity' in plant behaviour. He'd be happy with just that acknowledgement, but it doesn't come in any 'normal' way for there is no 'conversation', after all.

And hence the ultimate frustration, the lack of dialogue in this relationship, the near desperate need to know how the one you love feels about you. Bose is speaking for plant lovers like me when he says, 'If the plant could have been made thus to keep its own diary, then the whole of its history might have been recovered!'[178] It might have been this pent-up frustration that led Jagadish Bose to name his collection of essays *Awbyakto*, meaning the 'unsaid' in Bangla. The equivalence is easy to spot—Bose as plant, trying to articulate the unsaid. His famous essay, '*Gachher Kawtha*',[179] could mean two things,'The Story of Plants' and also, 'What Plants Say'. Bose begins with the fundamental question that plagued him all his life: 'Do plants say something?' Impatient with their lack of humanly comprehensible articulation, he begins by criticising our over-privileging of human speech over what might be considered tree speech.

We must get plants to write out their thoughts on paper, says Bose in this essay in Bangla. I paraphrase: There are so many countries and so many languages; why not the language of plants then? I concede that the civilised would be annoyed with this proposition, but there is no way out. And so Bose continues—it is a terribly passionate piece of writing, and even the cynic would be moved by his desire for the plant to write out its own 'autograph', and then an autobiography. Until this line arrives: 'It's our good fortune that the plant script is pretty close to the Devanagiri—it is difficult for the illiterate or the half literate to decipher'.[180]

'*Torulipi*', the script of plants—Bose even had a name for it. After telling us about a stringed instrument which could also double as a writing machine, Bose asks this question in a subheading: Are plants shy? He explains where his question is coming from—only the shy don't respond to our probing after all, just as plants don't verbally respond. What seems to hurt him the most is not that plants don't speak to him but that they cannot articulate their hurt—Bose ends up equating them with the deaf and dumb. The definition of life is a living creature's immediate response to physical hurt. His questions don't end: Does hurt excite a plant? How does a plant communicate its hurt to the rest of the world? How can that piece of communication be recorded? Will that record on paper give us a history of the plant?

But Bose and I were not the only members of the minority weird club that had wanted to communicate their love to trees through that extraordinary invention called the love letter. I was pleased, in the way one is, to discover long-lost relatives, to find that residents of Melbourne in faraway Australia had been writing romantic letters to their favourite trees since 2013. This is how one such letter went, for instance:

> My dearest Ulmus,
>
> As I was leaving St. Mary's College today I was struck, not by a branch, but by your radiant beauty. You must get these messages all the time. You're such an attractive tree.

This had been written to a green-leaf elm. Was the letter writer a nut like me?

No, there were several like him, according to *The Atlantic*.[181] Originally begun as an initiative by Melbourne's Environment Portfolio to 'make it easier for citizens to report problems like dangerous branches', it soon turned out that people had begun writing extra-official messages to the trees, 'everything from banal greetings and questions about current events to love letters and existential dilemmas', as Councillor Arron Wood reported.

The love letters were—for want of a better word—sweet. 'You're very pretty,' said one letter writer to an Algerian Oak; I wished to know what the oak thought of that compliment. The administration in Melbourne, aware of the human frustration with one-sided communication, set out to redress this by ventriloquating on behalf of the trees—so, some letter writers were lucky to get replies. This one is a good example:[182]

> To: Willow Leaf Peppermint, Tree ID 1357982
>
> 29 January 2015
>
> Hello Mr Willow Leaf Peppermint, or should I say Mrs Willow Leaf Peppermint?
>
> Do trees have genders? I hope you've had some nice sun today.
>
> Regards,
>
> L

The next day, the 30th of January, 2015, L found this reply:

> Hello
>
> I am not a Mr or a Mrs, as I have what's called perfect flowers that include both genders in my flower structure, the term for this is Monoicous. Some tree species have only male or female flowers on individual plants and therefore do have genders, the term for this is Dioicous. Some other trees have male flowers and female flowers on the same tree. It is all very confusing and quite amazing how diverse and complex trees are.
>
> Kind regards, Mr and Mrs Willow Leaf Peppermint (same Tree)

This is also a good reminder of the gender of the love letter, and not of the letter writer alone. (In case it needs reminding, '*patra*' is male and '*chitthi*' female in Hindi, both the words meaning 'letter'.) This exchange of letters, and the discourse, also brings to the surface the privileging of the love letter's presumed heterosexuality. For when one writes to a tree, how is one to address it? There, I said 'it'—how many of us are willing to think of a loved one as genderless?

'When you write to a friend, your letter should be a true picture of your heart, the style loose and irregular,' wrote H. W. Dilworth in his 1758 guide, *The Familiar Letter*

Writer. '(T)he thoughts themselves should appear naked, and not dressed in the borrowed robes of rhetoric; for a friend will be more pleased with that part of a letter which flows from the heart, than with that which is more a product of the mind.'[183] Reading this more than two and a half centuries after it was written, and noticing, of course, how the urges remain unchanged, I wondered, not for the first time, what a tree might make of those sentiments.

'Dear 1037148,' wrote one admirer to a golden elm in Melbourne. 'You deserve to be known by more than a number. I love you. Always and forever.'

Are we to offer a lover's discourse to a tree or a 'naked' love letter?

Love and the City

DIDIER COSTE

When the editor of this volume asked that I contribute an essay, she explained that 'love' could be taken here in any one of its many definitions, aspects and interpretations, or even several of them at once. As a practitioner of the love sonnet, a reader of Savitri, and an analyst of Spanish popular romance, I was tempted at first to limit my treatment of the topic to sentimental and erotic love. Indeed, these two kinds of love, that are often one and the same, will be at the heart of this brief sketch. Nevertheless, 'love' must also be historically and geographically contextualized; and thus this literary, cultural and global exploration of love and the city, or cities, through space and time.

The modern city (the city being modern by definition, even when it is ancient) anchors human love temporally and spatially in very distinctive ways. Not only does it provide a backdrop for the amorous experience, as the first landscapes (of hills and villages) that re-appeared in the European Renaissance after a long parenthesis to situate figures of saints or biblical stories in familiar settings and thus bring these closer to the beholder's life experience, but it also determines the possibilities and impossibilities, the conditions and stages of an amorous pursuit, the opportunities that favour it and the obstacles to its durability and success. For this reason, in the tragic love category, the plot of Shakespeare's *Romeo and Juliet* contrasts heavily with the medieval episodic structure of all *Tristan and Iseult* or *Lancelot and Guinevere* stories. Whatever happens in Verona is conditioned by the street and the *piazza*, the proximity of noble houses, the existence or not of secret and secluded places within walled city limits, balconies and dance halls, bedrooms with open doors and sacristies with closed ones. The (inefficient) speeches of the prince repeatedly invoke civil concord and citizenry, not feudal allegiance or God's law and will. A secular order of the *polis* is still to be established, but it is adumbrated, wished and called for as a remedy and a substitute for the shortcomings of providence. The modern city is becoming a parallel object of attachment, desire, nostalgia or repulsion, a rival for God and the rulers, a mirror of the beloved or an antagonist for the lover. It can be heavily anthropomorphized and even gendered, its feminine grammatical gender in Latin, Romance languages and German (*Stadt*) making it easier for the male gaze to frame and fantasize its femininity, whether as a whore, a courtesan, a femme fatale or a mother; hence Rastignac's famous war-cry when he plans to 'conquer' Paris. But, if the city replaces the ballroom, the walled garden and the alcoves of the castle or the dales of the pastoral genre, it does not do it at once: from Rousseau's *New Héloïse* (1761) to Alain Fournier's *The Grand Meaulnes* (1913) through Balzac's *The Lily of the Valley* (1834) and Emily Brontë's *Wuthering Heights* (1847), romantic, passionate love, associated with the primeval forces of nature, seems to wage a rearguard struggle against its corruption by the artificiality and complexity of city life. Thomas Hardy's *Far from the Madding Crowd* (1874) could be seen as an illustration of this tension.

In French literature, the decisive turn is sanctioned, a few years after Balzac's *Human Comedy*, by the two most celebrated literary works of the mid-nineteenth century, Baudelaire's *Flowers of Evil* and Flaubert's *Madame Bovary*. These two books, both published in 1857, with the addition of the 'Parisian Sketches' section to Baudelaire's work in 1861, remain highly influential within literature on love and the city through very different or even opposite currents, realist, naturalist, expressionist, experimental and formalist, or yet in surreal fantasies, both in France and far from it. Obvious traces of this turn can be found in Dos Passos and Donleavy, in Döblin and Eduardo Mendoza as well as in Apollinaire, Breton, Sartre, Cortázar, or, just the same in low grade novels and movies for popular consumption. The city is a playground for male hunters and female coquettes, for equivocal and fluid identities; it combines the qualities of a jungle where anything can happen, with those of a desert where the subject experiences total loneliness and the dream creatures or other fascinating figures that may appear and vanish instantly, like hallucinatory mirages, fabrications of some demon or devil.

The various English translations I could find of Baudelaire's sonnet 'À une passante' ('To a Passer-by') fail to account for some essential features outlined above. For example, the verb 'hurler' in the first line, '*La rue assourdissante autour de moi hurlait*' has been translated either as 'roar' or as 'thunder', when it should be 'howl' or at least 'yell': 'Around me, the deafening street howled,' like a jackal, a monkey or a mad human in a furious fit. The street is not 'natural,' it is at the same time savagely physical and an anti-physis, it is itself a living dead. The beautiful passer-by is a tall, slender and elegant widow; deadly attractive, she is a knowing temptress who darkly flashes more than she passes, she can only be dated in another world, a timeless afterworld, eternity. The difference between the previous 'bel inconnu' and 'belle inconnue' of medieval literature and the metropolitan passer-by is that the city lady or gentleman is not to be found there but to be *lost*. Robbe-Grillet, even in his attempt to caricature the Romantic topos, took it up very movingly in his 1963 film and cine-novel *L'Immortelle* ('The Immortal One').[184]

In *Madame Bovary*, Gustave Flaubert's provocative novel about a doctor's wife who has adulterous affairs, there are two cities, one provincial and not very large—Rouen, the only reachable horizon for country town, village dwellers and farmers; the other, Paris, a myth of which Rouen is only a small scale imitation or an incomplete suggestion. Emma will never visit Paris any more than exotic countries. Her two successive lovers will not take her away: they use her on the spot, to eat here. Rouen plays the role of the city by default and does not do it very well. It is too small to hide adulterous relations easily; it is too close to the rural roots and abodes of the protagonists (let us not forget that Emma's maiden name is Rouault) to escape a banal destiny. As a port, a historical place, one where there are theatres, hotels, restaurants and brothels, and shops that sell objects from the colonies, it exhibits an exotic façade, the tokens of adventure. Yet it is not the 'real thing'. When Emma and Léon start having a sexual affair, at the beginning of their second period, years after the squire Rodolphe has abandoned Emma, and briefly enjoy the blissful reflected delusion of a shared romantic passion, it is always associated with the natural, the elemental, not urban landscapes within city bounds. Amorous exaltation, however delicate, refined even in a second-hand fashion, will remain associated with flowers, the vegetal world, water and islands, as it was initially linked to the rural environment when Emma had married Charles, and to the brutality of the forest when she had been taken by Rodolphe. Inside the hotel room used as a love nest, the outdoor is reconstructed; love here is definitely an *exos* that the city, as it is, cannot fully represent:

> They were at the Hotel-de-Boulogne, on the harbour; and they lived there, with drawn blinds and closed doors, with flowers on the floor, and iced syrups were brought them early in the morning. Towards evening they took a covered boat and went to dine on one of the islands.[185]

Green leaves, grass, rain and sunrays, the motion of the branches under the wind, not domesticity, will forever remain fundamental constituents of Emma's eroticism as well as of its disappointment and guilt. Even the painted trees on the opera stage for *Lucy of Lamermoor*, 'that shivered when someone walked,' are part and parcel of it, and it seems that the false hopes she had on the day of her marriage were generated by 'walking to church, on the little path in the middle of the wheat fields.' In short, it is very difficult for the city to take over and replace the pagan setting for erotic love established since time immemorial, the idylls and eclogues of Ancient Greece, *Daphnis and Chloe*, the Renaissance pastoral, etc. The *hortus conclusus* of the secret but shameless union of bodies and souls will still be a garden, a park of Eden, a piece of pre-human world torn from the Creation to validate the pleasure of a primitive evasion, an easy if illusory instant return to the Golden Age: Luxembourg, Bois de Boulogne, Retiro, Hyde Park, Lodi Gardens, the Maidan, Prater or Central Park… it does not matter. These open spaces, across latitudes, are all the more open to positive feelings and vicarious fulfilment because they are enclosed within the dense hardness of city buildings.

Similarly, we can remember how the bus in which the couple of *Subida al paraíso* (*Ascension to Heaven*), one of Luis Buñuel's Mexican films, gives free rein to their passion, transforming into a tropical glasshouse when they make love. Or Wilhelm Jensen's short story Gradiva (1903), made famous by Freud's analysis and commentary published in 1907: in the bedrooms of Pompei, eighteen centuries ago, Roman couples were caught, trapped and frozen into carbonized statues right in the rapture of coitus; Gradiva could not be recognized as Zoe in a German city, but Zoe will eventually be recognized as Gradiva in the open air of the ruins of Pompei, where the ambitious city was destroyed by telluric forces.[186] Not much later, Proust's narrator in his young years experiences his first erotic stirring (and chilling) when he has a glimpse of Gilberte in her garden through a hole in the hedge. He will be drawn to Albertine near the sea, among the 'little bunch of blooming teen-agers.' Odette will be remembered as a beautiful lady at the Bois de Boulogne; this is where all the manoeuvring of the finest Parisian seduction takes place, it is where the enchanted past of young desire could briefly be revived many years later in the colours of autumn creepers. But Swann's jealousy and every cheated lover's despair require a décor of mineral streets, closed shutters, intense traffic or crowded railway stations.

Is the city an impossible presentness meant for sentimental as well as moral loss, the loss of innocence and sometimes the effacement of desire itself? Is the modern city, in the literary imagination as in some kinds of naturistic ecological discourses (that became articulate in the European mid-eighteenth century and perhaps culminated with Thoreau) a man-made Hell, the manifestation of a second Fall? Is it or should it be hated for this reason, or can it be loved solely in a perverted, Baudelairian way, for its sins and its cynicism? Or can it be synonymous with opportunities for unlimited encounters, boundless curiosity, a mirror of the depths and wonders of a liberated, unfettered, limitless self, or a mirror and a double of the beloved in its full otherness and its always renewed familiarity?

In fact, there are many ways and many reasons for incriminating Babylon, Sodom and Gomorrah, the imaginary cities of the plain, peopled by lone babblers, sodomites and gonorrheans. Too many (prosperous) people in one place are a crowd, too many piled up stones no longer make a humble temple. The city is a figure of excess to be regulated, straightened and divided into square plots by a stern *logos* instead of being ruled by chance and fantasy, lest it change into a labyrinth where bestiality and incest will reign. The city, then, can be loved or hated as a central superego (Metropolis) or, conversely, hated or loved as a gigantic, inventive mess, a brothel or a delirious fair. At the antipodes of the univocal simplicity of *ager*, its *forum, agora* or *maidan* is always dual: a place to celebrate order and unleash revolutions, the porch of the temple and the antechamber of decadence. There is August's Rome and Nero's Rome, the Pope's Rome and Fellini's *Roma*. This doubleness or duplicity explains why the city breeds doubles and forges identities, why, with urbanization, the spirits of the forest have moved downtown from the castle, the hollow trees and the village graveyard. Once the umbilical cord is broken with 'Mother Nature', body and spirit start a relentless fight: either you raise yourself to the top of one of the seven hills (those of Rome, or later of Constantinople) or you wallow in the marshes and markets of *down*town, if you don't carry out your dirty business underground, as in Eugene Sue's *Mysteries of Paris*, probably because, coming to the city from afar, Neville Landless, of *Edwin Drood* fame, could be anybody's name.

The city, therefore, will often be idealized from afar, by and for those who, not dwelling there, can enjoy sightseeing, on screen, on the printed page or as detached holidaymakers and honeymooners. 'Rome, by all means, Rome!'[187] is the place where a princess can briefly ride a scooter with a perfect stranger, and you, the movie-goer, can be this lucky stranger. You can be safely in love in and with Paris, Rome, Venice or New York, or even London, maybe, as long as you do not reside there, you don't get hooked and it is only an affair that you will remember gratefully, shedding a few rapidly dried tears: this is Hemingway's posthumous tale *A Moveable Feast* (1964) translated into French as *Paris est une fête*. The city—especially European cultural capitals (Paris, London, Vienna...) with their clichéd Bohemian life—has been eternally young in art, literature and showbiz, ever since Henri Murger's *Scènes de la vie de bohème* (1851) purported to describe the advantage of being a poor young artist or intellectual in nineteenth-century Paris. There followed Puccini's opera *La bohème* (1896), several films by King Vidor (1926), Marcel L'Herbier (1945) Aki Kaurismäki (1995), etc., and Charles Aznavour's world-famous song 'La bohème' of 1965: in the latter, the speaker is no longer young and regrets a 'time that those under twenty cannot imagine' in the same spirit as his equally nostalgic 'The Happy Days'. In other terms, the city is the same age as the artist and the ephemeral companion—'*midinette*' (a seamstress) or '*lorette*' (an 'easy' girl, maintained by more or less wealthy students)—of his youth; later on it becomes the ever-fresh memory of a merry mistress. François Truffaut's several 'Antoine Doinel' Parisian films shot between 1968 and 1979, with Jean-Pierre Léaud in the role of a young, then not so young adult thus hesitate between light-heartedness and disenchantment.

Only the stereotypes of light romantic comedy can perpetuate indefinitely the wonders of bumping into each other on Times Square or the Champs Élysées, or fighting for a cab and ending up in bed together for the weekend. We will find such features in the execrable TV series and films *Sex and the City* of the twenty-first century, also screened in an equally execrable, mechanical French dubbing. New York becomes a 'modernized,' culturally translated version of the early twentieth century Paris invented by Hollywood—without the quaint factor, replaced by business kitsch. A shift that echoes back in some French TV series, even in some episodes of the very popular *Plus belle la vie* ('Life is such a beauty'), located in Marseille, France's second largest city, a series that was initially supposed to emulate the Londonian *East Enders*. French and American moving pictures, increasingly in love with each other, have forgotten the lovers in the scripts. The neo-realist Italian film-makers of the '50s, on the contrary, were obsessed by them in the anthology of shorts *L'amore in città* (1953) that begins with the still shots of an 'inquiry' by Michelangelo Antonioni into the despair of relationships that lead to suicidal temptations. Satyajit Ray's tense and sober *Mahanagar*, entirely set in Calcutta ten years later, will probably seem truer to life now insofar as it breaks off with the sequels of nineteenth century melodrama. The modern city is loved as a go-between, and abhorred when it is made responsible for a divorce (the hectic life, dire economic realities, the quest of success or the appetite for new pleasures and pains stimulated by unlimited offer).

But are these *topoï* as constant as the modern association between love and the city, and truly universal? Let us have a quick look at some city fictions outside Europe and North America: Buenos Aires with Ernesto Sábato; Istanbul with Orhan Pamuk; Sydney with Peter Carey and 'Jacques Voisin', and Delhi with Khushwant Singh. We shall see that sudden, anarchic, huge and unprepared urban development, with uncontrolled rural migration and wild encounters between the old and the new, the local and the foreign, archetypes and the nuances of a harsh reality bring a vast diversity and some surprising vistas to our panorama.

It is remarkable that Sábato's generally admired and much commented novel *Of Heroes and Tombs* (1961), situated in the capital city of Argentina has attracted comparatively little critical attention about its treatment of Buenos Aires and what it has to do with sex, love and love-hate relationships. Not so with its imitation by Carlos Ruiz Zafón, the best-seller *La sombra del viento* ('The Shadow of the Wind'), 2001: Zafón even published an illustrated guidebook to the Barcelona of the novel! It may be that Argentinian criticism takes it wrongly for granted that Buenos Aires is emblematic of the totality of the politics, history and territory of the country. But, given that the only book on the topic is an archaeological study of the old mansion, now entirely torn down and replaced by a new building, that served as a model for the fictional house of Fernando Vidal Olmos and his daughter Alejandra, there are more interesting twists to this story. Firstly, the central point of the fictional space is an elevated *mirador*, where the final drama takes place, at the other vertical end of the subterranean, imaginary world in which, according to Fernando, the Secret Society of the Blind elaborates its dark designs. Secondly, the city world is divided in class terms like each of the three protagonists is morally and psychologically split: Alejandra has been a victim of rape and incest by her aristocratic father since she was a child, she eventually shoots him and burns herself alive; Martín, who, true to the *topos*, met Alejandra in Buenos Aires's emblematic Lezama park, is the fatherless son of a woman from the street, too lost or too shy to rescue Alejandra. Buenos Aires in Sábato's key novel, and in the whole trilogy, is cleft in every possible way; it is a disputed site between real and possible worlds and does not succeed in forming a unitary human space. In this sense, it can be interpreted as saying that there is *no* love in the city, because the city reflects human nature turned against itself.

Although there exists a class barrier between Kemal and Füsun, the lovers of Pamuk's *The Museum of Innocence* (*Masumiyet Müzesi*, 2008) and the theme of the double and unstable identities is a recurrent feature in most of this author's fiction, as it was in Sait Faik Abasıyanık's short stories—under the different pretexts of alcoholism and homosexuality—this border does not separate people and neighbourhoods as radically as it does in Sábato's work or in many realistic and naturalistic late nineteenth and twentieth century novels. Alternative, more socially suitable pairings, Kemal, the rich businessman, with his initial fiancée, the equally wealthy Sibel, and Füsun, the shop assistant, with an equally humble husband, fail badly after some years: Istanbul, the sacred core of Pamuk's world, cannot be divided into halves that remain physically alien to each other. Inner distance, the unachievability of intimacy except at the very moment of love-making, perhaps, is at the same time marked and compensated by voyeurism and fetishism. It could be said that Füsun, her family, her house, the furniture and objects therein, and, for the eight years of her married life, the joint portrait of a couple are all, separately and together, metonyms of a city that, from its two shores, obstinately resists separation, between old and new, East and West, high and low culture, land and sea, rich and poor, Islam and secularism, etc. The only attempt to leave it, aboard an old American convertible, turns into a foreseeable tragic ending, expected by the reader but not by the protagonist, when Füsun, after a night of intense love-making with Kemal, deliberately throws the car against a plane tree at the edge of the road (a repeat of Laale's oneiric elimination in Robbe-Grillet's film and cine-novel of 1963, *L'Immortelle*, also set in Istanbul). Repetition, obsession, museal preservation as a copy of life are characteristic of an attachment to the built 'patrimony' that entails a sanctuarized vision of the city, a citadel, the seat of divine and human power, whether it contains a palace, a cathedral, a mosque or a mandir. Kemal, who survives the accident, forms the project of creating a 'Museum of Innocence' that will reconstruct precisely the materiality of bliss, delegating it to every object, piece of furniture, utensil or even literally consumable product of the time, including a wall composition of cigarette butts. Orhan Pamuk has done it in real life, a hyperrealist installation of the fiction of the real, at the heart of the city. With this fiction and its own fetishization, we are already coming close, if in a rather perverse, oblique manner, to a love *of* the city that would no longer compete but identify harmoniously with a definite human object of love, an actual person with their full specificity and admired, or at least respected, irreducible otherness.

This is a feature whose emergence we can notice particularly well in successive novels of new world, immigrant cities, whether they were created from scratch by the European invader or they developed on a more or less ancient historical substratum. 'Love and the city' novels of New York range from *Sister Carrie* (1900) to Rushdie's extraordinary *Fury* (2001) through *Manhattan Transfer* (1925), but it seems nevertheless that in the mare magnum of New York city novels, love, in whatever sense, plays a minor part. Wall Street and the Bronx, at either end of Manhattan Island might explain it.

Thus I will turn first toward Sydney, due to the privilege of being allowed by some to consider myself as a Sydneysider. There are not so many urban novels of Sydney, discounting Marele Day's and Peter Corris's crime fiction. Sydney was rarely the subject matter of writers born in Sydney, such as Eleanor Dark or Christina Stead, who lived abroad for forty years and even moved the location of her *The Man who Loved Children* from Sydney to Washington in order to meet the expectations of the American readership. Conveniently, it leaves us at this time with only three fictions: Stead's *Seven Poor Men of Sydney* (1934), Peter Carey's *Oscar and Lucinda* (1988), and my own *Days in Sydney* (2005). As its title does nothing to hide, *Seven Poor Men* is a collection of working class lives, studied in an early neo-realist rather than a social realist vein, at the beginning of the twentieth century, and, although one woman, Catherine Baguenault, plays a key role in bringing together the seven men's lives, although her last name could also suggest it, she is not a flirtatious Snow White and she does not make it to the front-page. Among a multiplicity of incidents, 'love' is minimally scattered over several chapters from discovery to dissolution, and is only vaguely related to the city as such: 'The girls disappeared into the crowd. The boys blushed a little, laughed and went on.'[188] In *Oscar and Lucinda*, a candidate for the historical postcolonial label, bordering on the surreal, both protagonists are, in a sense, migrant misfits, these gamblers met by chance on the ship that brought them to Australia: she, an heiress, back from a year in England during which she could not find a husband, and he, turned Anglican missionary after abandoning his father's puritanical, austere and sadistic version of Christianity. The rejection of their bad manners by Sydney society, the exile to a faraway posting up north of Reverend Dennis Hasset who, in love with Lucinda, has unduly befriended her, and a protracted misunderstanding between the eponym protagonists will lead to the construction of a glass and cast iron church that Oscar brings to Hasset as a suicidal offering, until it dismantles on arrival. Sydney, not yet fully established, remains transitional, it appears as a displaced, circumstantial point of origin for the narrator, a ferment in time more than a *locus* of identity. With *Days in Sydney*,[189] a bilingual novel mainly situated in the 1980s, when the male protagonist, the Frenchman Jacques Voisin (who, ironically, signs his English poems on Port Jackson, published in *Poetry Australia* magazine, under the translated name James Neighbour) is, almost unknowingly after a long absence, in search of his estranged passionate love, Mathilda, the lonely Australian musician and painter of 'The Freudian Islands'. Mathilda has become a geography teacher and changed her name to Carol. Here, it is no longer a dragon that appears in the sky to a madman as in Sábato's Buenos Aires trilogy, but the face of the actual sun between the branches of Norfolk pines damaged by acid industrial pollution, a face that powerfully evokes Mathilda's blonde complexion and flowing golden hair, so close and yet an alien beauty. The two languages face to face, of the fully bilingual former lovers unite them and at the same time leave them separate and derelict, because they are headed in opposite directions. When Jacques discovers that his new young wife is Mathilda's niece and he is about to see her again at long last, he dies in a fatal car crash on a bridge, going home to his past *and* his present. In this novel, with its many hyperrealist everyday scenes and so-called secondary characters, the city of a new life, improbable but certain, becomes the object of a cult of the last chance; it becomes a complete, inescapable world, it holds the whole of Creation in itself.

So does, in a very different tone, Khushwant Singh's *Delhi*.[190] In its seven plus one incarnations, Delhi has apparently never been the right place for love. On what has almost constantly been a terrain of cruelty, massacres, alternately or concurrently ruled by raw power, corruption and hypocrisy that would invariably bring about its periodical destruction, culture and structures, masters and slaves, friends and foes would perish together. But, like a poetic phoenix or some primitive monstrous creature, it is also invariably re-generated from its complete fusion and confusion. Bhagmati, the character who co-presides, along with the narrator, over that sentimental journey through the ages, is transgender, a *hijra*, as the book is transgenre. The city of seven lives and destructions shuns identification. A complex of continuity in dysfunction, littered with the monuments of conquest, bloodshed and death or a brash casualty of uncontrolled modernization and unsustainable development, its beholder sees it under a new light every day, it is always the first time. Its endurance maintains or renews its endearment; it is the foundation of desire and responsibility, the possibility of change, transfer, reshaping and interpretation. Its historical narrativized memory is very similar in time to the relation between avatars in symbolic space. Afterlife and embodiment are crucial. Delhi is not a given *eidolon*, it is not reified, not a thing, therefore not a false god but a perpetually constructed and reconstructed, nearly present but unattainable object of desire, animated by the conjunction of its own will-to-be and persistence, and the lover's need for its concrete appearance, forever dissimilar to its idea. Bhagmati, a misfit, dark, ugly, transgressively attractive, is an anthropomorphic double of Delhi in almost every respect, including their self-destructive epileptic fits. The 'most vulgar', brutal and rudest whore in Delhi, according to the narrator, she is also sweet and protective, sensitive and able to cry like a little girl. Her name is that of a mythical, 'mystic' Hindu princess married to a Muslim sultan of a Southern Indian region at the end of the sixteenth century. Divided, but one and unique, she is her own 'wife', both ways. Neither of one conventional gender nor of the other, she is of both.

William Darlymple, in his *City of Djinns*, endeavours

to explain the condition and behaviour of modern *hijras* by 'the merging of the two traditions'[191] of eunuchs in Hindu and Muslim cultures, but he does not try to draw a link between their dual image of despicable barren devils and bountiful bearers of blessings for the newly wed, and the djinns, fearful ghosts, nasty *bhoot*s or the nicer elves that now haunt modern cities (including Gurgaon, they say) since there is nobody to feed them in the decrepit towers where the last locked-up princesses died of love-sickness and boredom when the first metro line opened in town, when the first crowd that had deserted the fields of Punjab or the Himalayan forests demonstrated on Janpath.

The djinns of Delhi, like the sunny but fleeting and unreachable face of Mathilda in Sydney, like her niece, a younger double, like all the doubles and substitutes we met in Pompei, Buenos Aires or Istanbul must also be interpreted as shy, incomplete returns of the repressed on the global stage of the city: each of them is a previous existence of mankind whose shape we blurred, a parent that we would like to believe in need of us, his or her unknown future, or yet the child we were in love with when we were children, whose name escapes us even when we suddenly recognize the eyes, the voice. From now on the city is the only place haunted by the other, our unknown, desirable alter ego; it is the new simulacrum of nature that we must love because there is no other.

Notes

1. Roland Barthes, *A Lover's Discourse: Fragments*. Published in 1977. Translated from French by Richard Howard. (Hill and Wang, 1978), p. 140.
2. Chela Sandoval, *Methodology of the Oppressed* (Minneapolis: University of Minnesota Press, 2000).
3. Barthes 1978, p. 142.
4. Debotri Dhar, "The Politics of Love and Marriage," *The Sunday Guardian*, September 17, 2016.
5. Debotri Dhar, 'Between *Sanskaras* and *Adhikaras*: Rape, Suicide, and the State.' Ph.D. dissertation. (New Brunswick: Rutgers University, 2013).
6. Debotri Dhar, *Just Love: Feminism, Faith and Intimate Violence* (Ann Arbor: Center for the Education of Women, 2016). For the phrase 'just love', I am indebted to feminist and religious ethicist Margaret Farley's book *Just Love: A Framework for Christian Sexual Ethics* (New York: Continuum, 2006).
7. Sharanya Manivannan, 'Boyfriend Like a Banyan Tree'. http://www.whiskeypaper.com/whiskeypaper/boyfriend-like-a-banyan-tree-by-sharanya-manivannan.
8. Ananya Vajpeyi, *Righteous Republic, The Political Foundations of Modern India* (Boston: Harvard University Press, 2012).

9. Ibid, p. 92.
10. Gloria Anzaldua, *Borderlands La Frontera* (San Francisco: Aunt Lute, 1987).
11. Bandana Tewari, "The Great Indian Wedding," *New York Times*, March 29, 2009.
12. http://www.girlsnotbrides.org/about-girls-not-brides/.
13. M.K. Gandhi, *Speeches and Writings of Mahatma Gandhi*, 1918, pp. 425-426. https://www.mkgandhi.org/indiadreams/chap55.html
14. Malashri Lal and Namita Gokhale, *In Search of Sita: Revisiting Mythology* (New Delhi: Penguin, 2009).
15. Sudhir Kakar, "Feminine Identity in India" in *Women in Indian Society: A Reader*, ed. Rehana Ghadially (Delhi: Sage, 1988).
16. Lal and Gokhale, *In Search of Sita*, p.126.
17. https://academiccommons.columbia.edu/download/fedora_content/.../1343169.pdf. Translated by Gayatri Chakravorty Spivak.
18. Patrick Olivelle, *Manu's Code of Law* (Oxford: Oxford University Press, 2005).
19. Chandrakala Padia, "Feminism, Tradition and Modernity: An Essay in Relation to Manusmriti" in *Feminism, Tradition and Modernity*, ed. Chandrakala Padia (New Delhi: Glorious Printers, 2002), pp. 208-216.
20. Raveendra Nath Yasarapu, "Divorce Rate in India," 1998. https://www.researchgate.net/post/The_divorce_rate_in_India_is_the_lowest_in_the_world_Is_the_Indian_way_of_life_a_model_for_Sustainable_living
21. Vikram Seth, *A Suitable Boy* (New Delhi: Penguin Viking, 1993).
22. Neelam Mulchandani, "Chitra Banerjee Divakaruni's *Arranged Marriage*: Multiple Consciousness and South Asian Diasporic Identity Formation". http://www.newmanpublication.com/issue/04%20Neelam%20Mulchandani.pdf

23. Rabindranath Tagore, "Streer Patra" (The Wife's Letter). https://www.parabaas.com/translation/database/translations/stories/gStreerPatra1.html See also Malashri Lal, "Tagore, Imaging the Other: Reflections on *The Wife's Letter* and *Kabuliwala*," https://www.dlib.si/stream/URN:NBN:SI:DOC-XOFJ4COQ/2454e01c-a6f2.../PDF
24. Chitra Banerjee Divakaruni, *The Palace of Illusions* (Picador, 2008).
25. https://www.theguardian.com/film/2001/sep/14/bollywood.artsfeatures. Accessed September 13, 2001.
26. Sunil Khilnani, *Incarnations: A History of India in Fifty Lives* (Farrar, Straus and Giroux, 2016).
27. Several scholars attest to the importance of the feminine aspect of God in Hindu traditions. See David Kinsley's introduction to *Hindu Goddesses: Visions of the Divine Feminine in the Hindu Religious Tradition* (Berkeley: University of California Press, 1986); see also John Hawley's Prologue to *Devi: Goddesses of India* (1–3) in *The Divine Consort: Radha and the Goddesses of India*, ed. John Stratton Hawley and Donna Marie Wulff (Berkeley: Graduate Theological Union, 1982.) In the opening lines of "The Divine Feminine in the Theology of Krishna" Graham M. Schweig declares: 'Nowhere in the panorama of world religious traditions, from ancient times to the present, do we find such a strong presence of the feminine voice within the divinity as we do in the Hindu complex of religion.' (441) See Graham M. Schweig, "The Divine Feminine in the Theology of Krishna," in *Krishna: A Sourcebook*, ed. Edwin F. Bryant (New York: Oxford University Press, 2007), p. 441. Kinsley's fifteen-page overview in *Hindu Goddesses* (81-94) analysing Radha in terms of 'The Gopi Tradition,' 'Radha as Belonging to Another (*Parakiya*),' and 'Radha as Belonging to Krsna (*Svakiya*),' remains one of the best introductions to her.

28. An earlier version of this essay was presented at the workshop on 'Radha: Transformation from Gopi to Goddess,' organized by Professor Harsha V. Dehejia of Carleton University, Ottawa, at the School of Arts and Aesthetics, Jawaharlal Nehru University, January 29-30, 2010 and published in the volume edited by him, *Radha: From Gopi to Goddess* (New Delhi: Niyogi Books, 2014), pp. 87-104.
29. See Jessica Frazier, "Bhakti in Hindu Cultures," in *The Journal of Hindu Studies*, Volume 6, Issue 2, August 1, 2013, pp. 101–113. Invoking Zizek and Kristeva, Frazier argues that Radha, the gopi-turned-Goddess, trades in her subjection for passionate commitment, incorporating both her divine lover and the audience into her purposive agency. For Frazier, she is a model of a strong, rather than weak, woman. Frazier, thus, makes a persuasive case against the conventional view that 'Even in *srngara*, the erotic mode, there is no notion of equality between devotee and deity. The function of this rasa is primarily to spiritualize and aestheticize male dominance of gender relations. In the numerous legends about Krishna's sexual adventures among the milkmaids *(gopis)* of Vraj, the initiative is always his to seduce, dally with, and desert his female partners...This implies, among other things, the passivity of the female.' (Quoted in Ranajit Guha, ed. *Subaltern Studies* VI (New Delhi: Oxford University Press India, 1989), pp. 48-49. Guha called Bhakti 'an ideology of subordination par excellence' (p. 259).
30. Charlotte Vaudeville, "Krishna Gopala, Radha, and the Great Goddess," in *The Divine Consort: Radha and the Goddesses of India*, ed. John Stratton Hawley and Donna Marie Wulff (Berkeley: Graduate Theological Union, 1982), p. 7.
31. Guy L. Beck, *Alternative Krishnas: Regional and Vernacular*

Variations on a Hindu Deity (Albany: SUNY Press, 2005), p. 72.

32. Barbara Stoller Miller, "Radha: Consort of Krsna's Vernal Passion," *Journal of the American Oriental Society*, Vol. 95, No. 4 (Oct.–Dec., 1975), p. 655.
33. Ibid, p. 668.
34. Ibid, p. 669.
35. Charlotte Vaudeville, "Evolution of Love-Symbolism in Bhagavatism," *Journal of the American Oriental Society* 82 (1), 1962, pp. 31-40.
36. Barbara Stoller Miller, "Radha: Consort of Krsna's Vernal Passion," *Journal of the American Oriental Society*, Vol. 95, No. 4 (Oct.–Dec., 1975), p. 670.
37. Miller, p. 655.
38. Kinsley, pp. 82-83. Kinsley mostly relies on Miller's Introduction (pp. 25-36) to *The Love Song of the Dark God*, Miller's translation of the *Gitagovinda*.
39. David Kinsley's introduction to *Hindu Goddesses: Visions of the Divine Feminine in the Hindu Religious Tradition* (Berkeley: University of California Press, 1986), p. 82.
40. Ibid.
41. Miller, op. cit.
42. Valerie Ritter, "Epiphany in Radha's Arbor," in *Alternative Krishnas: Regional and Vernacular Variations on a Hindu Deity*, ed. Guy L. Beck (Albany: State University of New York Press, 2005), p. 180.
43. For an interesting interpretation of *Gitagovinda* in Hindi, see Vidya Nivas (Bharatiya Jnanpith, 2005.)
44. Beck, p. 180.
45. Nimbarka (c. 13th century C.E.) instated the worship of Radha-Krishna long before Chaitanya. According to the *Sri Navadwipa-dham Mahatmya*, a later Chaitanyite text, he saw Sri Gauranga, the combined form of Radha and Krishna, who would later incarnate as Chaitanya, in a

vision. Later practitioners of Radha-Krishna worship, through such back projection and invention, tried to lend continuity and depth to their tradition.

46. See Ramakanta Rath's *Sri Radha* (Delhi: Har Anand, 1996). Rath, speaking of how he came to write the poem, reminisces, 'I reflected on who else could have experienced this kind of emotion—love and terror in equal measure. I decided that it could be only one person, Radha,' (Quoted in Hariharan Balakrishnan, *The Hindu Literary Review,* 2 April 2006). Rath's Radha is not simply Krishna's beloved, but is endowed with a subjectivity that is independent and strong, not merely relational.
47. Graham M. Schewig, "The Divine Feminine in the Theology of Krishna," in *Krishna: A Sourcebook*, ed. Edwin F. Bryant (New York: Oxford University Press, 2007), p. 458.
48. See Bihari Lal, *The Satasaī*, trans. Krishna P. Bahadur (New Delhi: Penguin Books, 1992.)
49. I owe thanks to Dr. Imre Bangha of the faculty of Oriental Studies, Oxford University, for his help in understanding this couplet.
50. Vidya Nivas Mishra, *Radha Madhav Rang Rangi* (Bharatiya Jnanpith, 2005.)
51. I refer to Bihari Lal, *The Satasaī*, trans. Krishna P. Bahadur (New Delhi: Penguin, 1992.)
52. Valerie Ritter, "Epiphany in Radha's Arbor," in *Alternative Krishnas: Regional and Vernacular Variations on a Hindu Deity*, ed. Guy L. Beck (Albany: State University of New York Press, 2005), p. 180.
53. 'Jagat,' http://jagadanandadas.blogspot.in/search/label/radha, accessed 17 August 2012.
54. Jayadeva, *Gita Govinda: Love Songs of Radha and Krishna*, trans. Lee Siegel (New York: NYU Press, 2009), p. 121.
55. Ibid.
56. David Kinsley, *Hindu Goddesses: Visions of the Divine*

Feminine in the Hindu Religious Tradition (Berkeley: University of California Press, 1986), p. 93.

57. Ibid, p. 31.
58. Ibid.
59. Cheever Mackenzie Brown, *God as Mother: A Feminine Theology in India: An Historical and Theological Study of the Brahmavaivarta Purana* (Virginia: C. Stark, 1974), p. 179.
60. Kinsley, *Hindu Goddesses*, p. 94.
61. Ibid.
62. Sures Banerji, *A Companion to Tantra* (Delhi: Abhinav Publications, 2007), p. 134.
63. Ibid, p. 135.
64. Ibid, p. 189.
65. Guy L. Beck, *Alternative Krishnas: Regional and Vernacular Variations on a Hindu Deity* (Albany: SUNY Press, 2005), p. 71.
66. Ibid, pp. 71-72.
67. Jayadeva, *Gita Govinda: Love Songs of Radha and Krishna*, trans. Lee Siegel (New York: NYU Press, 2009), pp. 178-179.
68. Ibid, p. 160.
69. Ibid, p. 137.
70. Ibid, pp. 41-42.
71. Susie Tharu and K. Lalita, *Women Writing in India: 600 B.C. to the Present* (New York: Feminist Press, 1993).
72. Edwin F. Bryant, "Krishna in the Tenth Book of the Bhagavata Purana," In *Krishna: A Sourcebook*, ed. Edwin F. Bryant (New York: Oxford UP, 2007), p. 131.
73. https://theblog.okcupid.com/race-and-attraction-2009-2014-107dcbb4f060
74. http://www.thehindu.com/data/just-5-per-cent-of-indian-marriages-are-intercaste/article6591502.ece
75. https://www.theguardian.com/world/2016/jul/09/india-love-revolution-dating-fun-arranged-marriage-apps-tinder

76. https://qz.com/1198086/india-has-a-new-caste-for-native-english-speakers-only/
77. https://www.thehindubusinessline.com/blink/cover/Love-in-the-time-of-Tinder/article20921199.ece
78. http://theladiesfinger.com/is-tinder-the-harbinger-of-a-dating-apocalypse-or-are-we/
79. https://www.dailyo.in/lifestyle/single-women-sex-in-india-casual-sex-dating-app-one-night-stand-marriage-relationships/story/1/21848.html
80. http://theladiesfinger.com/sex_it_gets_better/
81. https://www.tandfonline.com/doi/abs/10.1080/19472498.2015.1109306? journalCode=rsac20
82. http://roundtableindia.co.in/index.php?option=com_content&view=article&id=8748:dalit-identity-or-commodity-for-savarnas&catid= 119:feature&Itemid=132
83. http://www.dalitweb.org/?p=736
84. https://www.dailyo.in/lifestyle/single-women-sex-in-india-casual-sex-dating-app-one-night-stand-marriage-relationships/story/1/21848.html
85. https://roundtableindia.co.in/index.php?option=com_content&view=article&id=8354:dalits-and-inter-caste-marriage&catid=119: feature&Itemid=132
86. https://thebodyisnotanapology.com/magazine/dear-queer-black-activists-an-honest-letter- about-desirability-politics-among-our-men/
87. In February 2016, Bharatiya Janata Party lawmaker Gyan Dev Ahuja from Rajasthan claimed that more than 10,000 cigarette butts, 4,000 beedis, 50,000 bone pieces, 2,000 wrappers 3,000 used condoms, 2,000 liquor bottles and 3000 beer cans are found daily at the JNU campus. (http://www.thehindu.com/news/national/3000-condoms-2000-liquor-bottles-at-jnu-this-bjp-mla-is-keeping-count/article8272367.ece)
88. http://www.globalresearch.ca/interview-with-osama-bin-laden-denies-his-involvement-in-9-11/24697

89. See for instance Urvashi Butalia, "Community, State and Gender: Some Reflections on the Partition of India," in *Women and the Politics of Violence*, ed. Taisha Abraham (Delhi: Haranand, 2002).
90. For a detailed discussion, refer to my book *Sikhs: The Untold Agony of 1984* (New Delhi: Westland, 2015).
91. Nilanjan Mukhopadhyay, *The Demolition: India At The Crossroads* (Delhi: HarperCollins, 1994), p. 305.
92. Ibid, p. 306.
93. Ibid.
94. Dibyesh Anand, *Hindu Nationalism in India and the Politics of Fear* (Palgrave Macmillan, 2011), pp. 64-5.
95. https://www.youtube.com/watch?v=-uN5GaQ41e8
96. Charu Gupta, *EPW*, December 19, 2009.
97. Some details of these have been provided in http://www.openthemagazine.com/article/nation/love-jihad & http://www.theguardian.com/world/2015/jan/29/love-jihad-india-one-man-quest-prevent-it
98. http://www.newskarnataka.com/mangalore/serial-killer-cyanide-mohan-kumar-convicted
99. http://www.hindujagruti.org/hindu-issues/love-jihad/history-of-love-jihad
100. [http://www.ndtv.com/india-news/the-mystery-of-kawwal-were-muzaffarnagar-riots-based-on-distortion-of-facts-534608]
101. http://www.wsj.com/articles/hindu-activists-in-india-warn-women-to-beware-of-love-jihad-1409874089
102. http://indianexpress.com/article/india/politics/bjp-unnao-mp-sakshi-maharaj-claims-madrasas-offering-cash-rewards-for-love-jihad/
103. http://indiatoday.intoday.in/story/love-jihad-meerut-woman-yogi-adityanath-bjp/1/395471.html
104. http://scroll.in/article/742851/has-the-bjp-imported-its-love-jihad-fear-mongering-into-bengal-with-the-tuktuki-mondal-case

105. http://organiser.org/Encyc/2014/8/30/40_05_17_06_editorial_H@@IGHT_162_W@@IDTH_319.jpg
106. http://panchjanya.com/Encyc/2014/8/30/41_03_24_23_love_jihad_Cover4_H@@IGHT_274_W@@IDTH_329.jpg
107. http://in.reuters.com/article/india-religion-modi-idINKBN0GZ2OC20140904
108. http://www.hindustantimes.com/Images/popup/2015/1/08_01_15-metro1d.jpg
109. http://indiatoday.intoday.in/story/love-jihad-oommen-chandy-islam-kerala-muslim-marriage/1/215942.html
110. https://thewire.in/law/supreme-court-sets-aside-kerala-hc-order-annulling-hadiya-marriage
111. https://indianexpress.com/article/india-others/kerala-bishop-accuses-hindu-outfit-of-love-jihad-by-abducting-catholic-girls-from-christian-faith/
112. For a general introduction to the subject of love in the Urdu ghazal, see Agnieszka Kuezkiewicz-Fras, "The beloved and the lover-love in the classical Urdu ghazal," *Cracow Indological Studies* Vol. XII (2010). For a more comprehensive engagement with the theme of love in South Asia from the perspective of literature, literary history, philosophy, social history, anthropology and film studies, see *Love in South Asia, A Cultural History*, ed. Francesca Orsini (New Delhi: Cambridge University Press, 2007).
113. In Persian and Urdu, *bastan* (Persian) or *bandhna* (Urdu), that is, 'to tie', 'to bind' is the metaphor for using a word or trope in poetry. This has been extremely elegantly stated by Ghani Kashmiri, the great Indo-Persian poet of the early seventeenth century:

    Aab buvad ma'ni-e raushan ghani
    khub agar bastah shaved gauhar ast

    A brilliant theme, oh Ghani, is bright water
    If it's bound well in a poem, it's a pearl.

114. *Ta'lil* means to provide a 'poetic' and unlikely reason or justification for an otherwise unremarkable fact.
115. *Zalim* can be a word of praise and admiration in Urdu in the appropriate context, as in the present verse of Ghalib's.
116. The notion that fair skin is a precondition for being considered beautiful entered Urdu poetry late in the nineteenth century. Ghalib's senior contemporary Shaikh Imam Bakhsh Nasikh (1773-1838) wrote:

    husn ko chahiye andaz-o ada naaz-o namak
    kya hua gar hui goron ki tarah khaal safed

    Beauty needs style, and elegance, and coquetry and piquant saltiness
    So what if someone had a hide, white like that of the white man?

    In ancient Arabia, the salt used was dark and the Arabic word for salt is *malh*; a dark, good-looking person was described as *malih* or 'salty'. This sense of 'salt,' and the word, was borrowed in Persian, then in Urdu. Urdu has both words *namkin* and *malih* for a good-looking, dark-complexioned person. Hence Nasikh requires *namak* or salt as a necessity for beauty. Note that I use the pejorative 'hide' in my translation because the poet has used the word *khaal* that has the same effect.
117. Gyan Chand Jain, *Tafseer-e Ghalib* (Srinagar: Jammu and Kashmir Academy of Art, Culture, and Literature, 1971.)
118. For an illuminating discussion on the subject see C. M. Naim, "The Theme of Homosexual Love in Pre-Modern Urdu Poetry," in M. U. Memon ed. *Studies in the Urdu Ghazal and Prose Fiction* (Madison: University of Wisconsin, 1979), pp. 120-42. Also see Ruth Vanita and Saleem Kidwai, eds., *Same-Sex Love in India: Readings from Literature and History* (New York, St. Martin's Press 2002).
119. For an excellent discussion of the poetics of love in the Urdu ghazal see Shamsur Rahman Faruqi, "The Conventions

of Love or the Love of Conventions: Urdu Love Poetry in the 18th century," *Annual of Urdu Studies*, Madison, Wisconsin, Vol. 14, 1999.

120. I want to express my gratitude to Anees Ayesha whose book *Urdu Poetry: An Introduction* (translated from Urdu into English by Zafar Anjum, and published by Kitaab, Singapore, 2013) provided the framework and material for much of this essay.
121. Edward Hirsch, *A Poet's Glossary* (Boston and New York: Houghton Mifflin Harcourt, 2014).
122. Anees Ayesha, *Urdu Poetry: An Introduction,* trans. Zafar Anjum (Singapore: Kitaab, 2013).
123. Ibid.
124. Zafar Anjum, *Iqbal: The Life of a Poet, Philosopher and Politician* (Vintage Books: Random House India, 2014).
125. Muhammad Sadiq, *A History of Urdu Literature* (Delhi: Oxford University Press, 1984).
126. Ibid.
127. Tanveer Alvi, *Urdu Mein Baramase ki Riwayat: Matalon Mein* (Delhi: Urdu Akademi, 1988).
128. Ibid.
129. See Francesca Orsini (ed.) *Before the Divide: Hindi and Urdu Literary Culture* (New Delhi: Orient Blackswan, 2010).
130. For details see Carla Petievich, *When Men Speak as Women* (New Delhi: Oxford University Press, 2007).
131. Afzal Jhinjhanavi, *Bikat Kahani*, Introduced by Nurul Hasan Hashmi and Masood Husain Khan (Lucknow: Idara Farogh-e-Urdu, 1970).
132. Tanveer Alvi, *Urdu Mein Baramase ki Riwayat: Matalon Mein* (Delhi: Urdu Akademi, 1988).
133. *LikeLoveQuotes.com* http://likelovequotes.com/11-things-that-mean-more-to-men-than-i-love-you/. Website accessed August 5, 2016.

134. Roland Barthes, *A Lover's Discourse: Fragments*, trans. Richard Howard (Hill and Wang, 1978).
135. In a 1967 essay titled 'The Death of the Author,' Roland Barthes argued that the author's own identity, experiences, and intent are irrelevant to literary interpretation; instead, the author is merely a 'scriptor,' and each text is re-written in the here and now with each re-reading by its audience.
136. Elaine Showalter, *A Literature of Their Own: British Women Novelists from Brontë to Lessing* (Princeton: Princeton University Press, 1977).
137. Joyce Carol Oates, "Is There a Female Voice? Joyce Carol Oates Replies" in *Feminist Literary Theory: A Reader*, ed. Mary Eagleton (Cambridge: Blackwell, 1986) pp. 208-209.
138. Debotri Dhar, *The Courtesans of Karim Street* (New Delhi: Niyogi, 2014).
139. Meha Pande, "Modern Day Courtesans," *The Pioneer*, October 18, 2015.
140. For a socio-historical analysis, see for instance Veena Oldenberg, "Lifestyle as Resistance: The Case of the Courtesans of Lucknow, India." *Feminist Studies* Vol. 16, No. 2, 'Speaking for Others/Speaking for Self: Women of Color' (Summer, 1990), pp. 259-287.
141. Rabindranath Tagore, *Ghare Baire*, in *Rabindra-Rachanabali* Volume 8 (Calcutta: Vishwabharati, 1941) pp. 141-334. English translation by Surendranath Tagore, *The Home and the World*, ed. Ajanta Dutt (Delhi: Doaba Publications, 2002).
142. Cynthia A. Leenerts, "Rabindranath Tagore's and Satyajit Ray's 'New Woman': Writing and Rewriting Bimala," in *Rabindranath Tagore: Universality and Tradition*, ed. Patrick Colm Hogan and Lalita Pandit (London: Associated University Presses, 2003); and Ashis Nandy, "The Novels: The Home and the World", in *The Home and the World*, trans. Surendranath Tagore, ed. Ajanta Dutt (Delhi: Doaba Publications, 2002).

143. Partha Chatterjee, "The Nationalist Resolution of the Women's Question," in *Postcolonial Discourses: An Anthology*, ed. Gregory Castle (Oxford: Blackwell Publishers, 2001), pp. 152-65.
144. Debotri Dhar, "Women, Homes, Histories: Main Trends in Modern Indian Literary Fiction," in *India: Histories of the Present,* ed. Saurabh Dube and Ishita Banerjee, *Istor* 59, Dec 2014.
145. Edna O'Brien, "Inner Cowboy," in *Saints and Sinners* (New York: Back Bay Books, 2011), pp. 103 -129.
146. Téa Obreht, *The Tiger's Wife* (New York: Random House, 2011).
147. Debotri Dhar, "Radha's Revenge: Feminist Agency, Postcoloniality and the Politics of Desire in Anita Nair's Mistress," *Postcolonial Text*, Vol 7, No 4 (2012).
148. Darren Richard Carlaw, http://www.nyjournalofbooks.com/book-review/postcards-oxford-stories-women-and-travel
149. bell hooks, *Art on my Mind: Visual Politics* (New York: The New Press, 1995), pp. 125-6.
150. The judgements garnered great praise, not least for their lyricism. Several judges referenced poets, from William Shakespeare to Leonard Cohen, and one even included a moving indication of regret. 'History owes an apology to the members of this community and their families, for the delay in providing redressal for the ignominy and ostracism that they have suffered through the centuries,' wrote Justice Indu Malhotra. It may be worth noting, however, that only a few paragraphs later, she also declared that her judgement against 377 should not 'lead to the reopening of any concluded prosecutions', which, even if legally sound, does rather negate the spirit of the suggested apology.
151. Dhananjay Mahapatra, "Constitution for equality, but Section 377 denies the right," *The Times of India*, 12 July 2018.

169. Ironically, this idea of an idyllic past is also used by supporters of Section 377 to argue that homosexuality itself is a 'foreign' import into India.
170. "Introduction," *Same-Sex Love in India: Readings in Indian Literature* (Palgrave Macmillan, 2000).
171. Mina Kumar, in "Lesbians in Indian Texts and Contexts," *Facing the Mirror: Lesbian Writing from India*, edited by Ashwini Sukthankar (New Delhi: Penguin, 1999).
172. 'As Rita, an upper middle-class woman from Mumbai remarked plaintively, "I just want to *be* gay, I don't want to attend conferences about it".' ("Introduction", *Facing the Mirror*)
173. Katie Holten, *About Trees* (Berlin: Broken Dimanche Press, 2015).
174. http://www.katieholten.com/AboutTrees.Prints.html
175. Address in Bangla to Students of Presidency College, Calcutta, February 25, 1917.
176. Quoted in *Jagadish Basu Rachana Sangraha*, ed. Arup Ratan Bhattacharjee and Sailen Chakraborty (Kolkata: Dey's Publishing, 2013).
177. Jagadish Basu, *Awbyakto (*Kolkata: Dey's Publishing, 2009), p. 123.
178. Ibid, p.127.
179. Quoted in *Jagadish Basu Rachana Sangraha*, ed. Arup Ratan Bhattacharjee and Sailen Chakraborty (Kolkata: Dey's Publishing, 2013).
180. Jagadish Basu, *Awbyakto*, p. 127. Translation mine.
181. http://www.theatlantic.com/technology/archive/2015/07/when-you-give-a-tree-an-email-address/398210/
182. Ibid.
183. H. W. Dilworth, *The Familiar Letter Writer* (New York: Gaine, 1761).
184. The male protagonist is constantly in search of a beautiful and mysterious Turkish woman who keeps on disappearing

and re-appearing in the crowds of Istanbul and whose death in a motor accident is repeated too often to be more than a dream fabrication. A seductive mistress who never reveals her identity, the lover is a female embodiment of the city of Istanbul/Constantinople/Byzantium.

185. http://www.planetpublish.com/wpcontent/uploads/2011/11/Madame_Bovary_NT.pdf p. 417

186. 'Gradiva' is the imagined name given by the German archaeologist Norbert Harold to a female figure depicted on a Roman bas-relief. Norbert becomes obsessed with it; in the German city where he lives, he fails to identify its resemblance with his young neighbour Zoe, but, in the open air of the ruins of Pompei, he will eventually recognize his Gradiva in the living Zoe, who has also travelled to the re-discovered ghost city, destroyed in 79 CE by a massive eruption of the Vesuvius volcano.

187. A famous profession of love placed in the mouth of Audrey Hepburn by William Wyler in his 1953 film *Roman Holiday*.

188. Christina Stead, *Seven Poor Men of Sydney* (Sydney: Angus & Robertson, 1990), p. 121.

189. Didier Coste, *Days in Sydney* (Paris: Noésis-Agnès Viénot, 2005).

190. Khushwant Singh, *Delhi, a Novel* (New Delhi: Penguin Books, 1990).

191. William Darlymple, *City of Djinns: A Year in Delhi*. (1993: New York-London-New Delhi: Penguin Books, 2003) p. 173.

Pande, Alka. *Shringara: The Many Faces of Indian Beauty*. New Delhi: Rupa Publications, 2011.

Pande, Alka. *Body Sutra*. New Delhi: Rupa Publications, 2019.

Pande, Alka. *Indian Erotica*. Roli Books, New Delhi, 2000.

Zimmer, H. *The Arts of Indian Asia: Myths and Symbols in Indian Art and Civilization*. Princeton: Princeton University Press, 1946.

Sinha, Indira. *Love Teachings of Kamasutra: With Extracts from Koka Shastra, Anaga Ranga and Other Famous Indian Works on Love*. Boston: Da Capo Press. 2008.

Vatsyayana. *The Kamasutra of Vatsyayana*. Translated by Sir Richard Burton & F. F. Arbuthnot. Ware: Wordsworth Classics, 1995.

Sudhir Kakar and Wendy Doniger. *Kamasutra*. Oxford: Oxford University Press. 2003.

About the Contributors

Zafar Anjum is a journalist and writer based in Singapore. He has authored *Kafka in Ayodhya and Other Short Stories* (Kitaab, 2015), *Startup Capitals: Discovering the Global Hotspots of Innovation* (Random House India, 2014), *Iqbal: The Life of a Poet, Philosopher and Politician* (Vintage Books/ Random House India, 2014), *The Resurgence of Satyam* (Random House India, 2012), and *The Singapore Decalogue: Episodes in the Life of a Foreign Talent* (Red Wheelbarrow Books, 2012).

Didier Coste is Professor Emeritus of Comparative Literature at Bordeaux-Montaigne University. He has researched and taught at many universities on all five continents and was twice a fellow of JNIAS, JNU, New Delhi. As a scholar, his best-known book is *Narrative as Communication* (Minnesota University Press, 1989), but he has published in several fields of literary and cultural theory. He initiated and chaired the Noesis International Cultural Foundation for the Arts and Literature (1983-1997). He is also an award-winning translator of narrative, poetry, and essays from Spanish and English into French and a bilingual poet and novelist. His last (bilingual) novel was *Days in Sydney*, Paris, 2005. His latest published poetry collection is *Indian Poems* (Writers Workshop, Kolkata, 2019).

Christina Dhanaraj is a Christian Dalit woman from Chennai, India. She is a consultant for women and minority-led initiatives focusing on social justice, self-determination, and collaborative models of scholarship. She is currently an advisor for Smashboard.

She was formerly a consultant for #dalitwomenfight and the co-founder of the Dalit history month project. She works and lives in the Netherlands.

Mehr Afshan Farooqi is an Associate Professor in the Department of Middle Eastern and South Asian Languages and Cultures at the University of Virginia, where she teaches a variety of courses on literature, culture, history and arts of the Indian subcontinent. She has published extensively on Urdu literary culture. Her books include *Urdu Literary Culture: Vernacular Modernity in the Writing of Muhammad Hasan Askari* (New York: Palgrave-Macmillan, 2012); *The Oxford India Anthology of Modern Urdu Literature*, volume one, poetry and miscellaneous writing (New Delhi: Oxford University Press, 2008) and *The Oxford India Anthology of Modern Urdu Literature*, volume two, fiction (New Delhi: Oxford University Press, 2008), among several others.

Rakhshanda Jalil is a translator, writer, and literary historian. She has published over twenty-five books and written over fifty academic papers and essays. Her most recent works include an edited volume of critical writings on Ismat Chughtai called *An Uncivil Woman* (Oxford University Press, 2017); and a literary biography of the Urdu poet Shahryar (HarperCollins); *The Great War: Indian Writings on the First World War* (Bloomsbury); *Preeto & Other Stories: The Male Gaze in Urdu* (Niyogi) and *Kaifiyat*, a translation of Kaifi Azmi's poems and *Jallianwala Bagh: Literary Responses in Prose &Poetry* (Niyogi Books) and most recently, *But You Don't Look Like a Muslim* (HarperCollins). She runs an organization called Hindustani Awaaz, devoted to the popularization of Hindi-Urdu literature and culture. She was awarded the Kaifi Azmi Award for her contribution to Urdu and the First Jawad Memorial Prize for Urdu-Hindi Translation. She writes regularly for major newspapers such as *Hindustan Times, Indian Express* and *The Hindu* as well as magazines such as *Outlook, Scroll* and *The Wire*. She is the Editor of the *Taj* magazine, the bi-annual book-length journal of the Taj group of hotels.

Malashri Lal recently retired from her position as Professor, Department of English, at the University of Delhi. She is a member of the English Advisory Board at the Sahitya Akademi, and also a member of Bharatiya Jnanpith's advisory committee. Her specialization is in Literature, Women and Gender Studies about which she has written fifteen books, including *In Search of Sita: Revisiting Mythology* (Penguin 2009, 2018), *Tagore and the Feminine: A Journey through Translations* (Sage, 2015) and *Finding Radha: The Quest for Love* (Penguin Random House, 2019). Malashri Lal has been a Senior Consultant to the Ministry of Culture, UGC nominee on Committees, and a member of international book award juries.

Nilanjan Mukhopadhyay is a Delhi-based print, television and news media journalist. His first book, *The Demolition: India At The Crossroads*, was published in 1994 and was written in the aftermath of the Babri Masjid's demolition. After working for almost two decades in a variety of media, including running a small media organisation, he published his second book, an acclaimed biography of Prime Minister Narendra Modi, in 2013. Thereafter, he wrote *Sikhs: Untold Agony of 1984* and *The RSS: Icons of the Indian Right*, in 2019. He also writes columns for several leading Indian papers and websites besides hosting a web-based video programme.

Alka Pande is an academic and a museum curator. She has been a Reader at the Department of Fine Arts, Panjab University, Chandigarh, from 1996 till 2000, prior to which she was Director of the Museum of Fine Arts, Panjab University. Since 2000, she has been Art Consultant at the India Habitat Centre, New Delhi. Pande has curated several shows in India and Europe, including 'Art in the Metro', an intiative by India Habitat Centre and Delhi Metro, and the Delhi Photo Festival, a biennial photography festival organized by the IHC and Nazar Foundation in Delhi. In October 2014, Pande curated 'The Kama Sutra: Spirituality and Eroticism in Indian Art' at Pinacotheque de Paris. From November 2010-February 2011, she was the curator of 'India Awakens:

Under the Banyan Tree' at the Essi Museum, Klostemeuburg, in Austria. Pande is the author of several books on Indian art and erotica, including *Masterpiece Of Indian Art* (2004), *A Celebration of Love: Myriad Moods of Love* (2004), and *Indian Erotica*, co-authored with Lance Dane (2002).

Makarand R. Paranjape is currently Director, Indian Institute of Advanced Study, Shimla. He was educated at St. Stephen's College, Delhi, and the University of Illinois at Urbana-Champaign, where he got his Masters and PhD in English. He has been Professor of English at Jawaharlal Nehru University for over twenty of his thirty-nine years as university teacher. He is the author of some twenty and editor of over two dozen books, in addition to hundreds of academic papers and popular articles. His latest books include *Swami Vivekananda: Hinduism and India's Road to Modernity* (HarperCollins, 2020), *New Perspectives in Indian Science and Civilization* (Routledge, 2020), *Debating the 'Post' Condition in India* (Routledge, 2018), and *The Death and Afterlife of Mahatma Gandhi* (Penguin Random House, 2015). Makarand is currently a columnist in *Open Magazine*, *Mail Today*, and *The Print*.

Sumana Roy is the author of *How I Became a Tree* (Aleph), a work of nonfiction, *Missing: A Novel* (Aleph), *Out of Syllabus: Poems* (Speaking Tiger), and *My Mother's Lover and Other Stories* (Bloomsbury). She teaches at Ashoka University.

Parvati Sharma is a Delhi-based author. Her debut collection of short stories was called *The Dead Camel and Other Stories of Love*, which explored love and sexuality in modern India. She has also written a novel, *Close to Home: A Historical Biography; Jahangir: An Intimate Portrait of a Great Mughal* and two books for children, *The Story of Babur* and *Rattu & Poorie's Adventures in History: 1857*. She has worked as a travel writer, editor and journalist, writes a column on books and history for *The Hindu Business Line*.